The Story of a S⋯ ⋯er

Being the Autob⋯ ⋯n
Auther⋯

Stanley Waterloo

Alpha Editions

This edition published in 2024

ISBN : 9789362927613

Design and Setting By
Alpha Editions
www.alphaedis.com
Email - info@alphaedis.com

Contents

INTRODUCTION

THE story that follows this introduction is literally true. There died lately, in a Western State prison, a man of the class known as habitual criminals. He was, at the time of his death, serving out a sentence for burglary. For thirty years he had been under the weight of prison discipline, save for short periods of freedom between the end of one term and the beginning of another.Because of this man's exceptional qualities, as contrasted with those of the multitude of criminals, he was induced, semi-officially, in a friendly way, to write the story of his life. He accepted the proposition made to him, though, consistent with his quality, not quite fulfilling his pledge, omitting, as he did, certain hard details of the later part of his criminal career. This was but natural, and, perhaps, it is the one incident which shows that the man realized, in some measure, the truth as to his own character.

The account which makes this book was written in 1897 and 1898, when its author was in the free world. It has been thought best, out of regard for an estimable family, to omit from the printed work the real name of the writer. Another name has been substituted for the actual one, but, with the exception of a few necessary technical corrections, and changes of names of people and of one vessel—the one in which the first voyage was made— the manuscript appears almost as it left the hands of its author.

As a true tale, as a study of sociology, as a picture of one human life somehow bent and twisted from the normal, this work, it seems to the editor, is one of the most surprising of productions. Its frank unconsciousness, its striking revelations, its absence from all pose, combine to make it unique among the writings of men. The Confessions of Rousseau appear, in phases, almost artificial compared with the simple but startling revelation which is here given.

It was not hopelessness, nor recklessness, nor penitence, which made this man write down unflinchingly what he remembered of the story of his life. A cheerful reminiscent vein runs throughout all he tells. His sense of humour is ever present. Nowhere appears a hint of the tragedy of his experience. Of that he was not conscious. He was as free from remorse and self-upbraiding as a wild animal or a tree.

The story, one would imagine, should appeal to those who think. From the beginning can be seen, in the character of the runaway sailor and one-time officer of the navy, traits which indicate his absolute failure, eventually, as a man. He drifts. He is irresponsible. He escapes from one dilemma only to get into another. He is thriftless, and takes no thought for the morrow. He has no regard for the truth, nor any for the rights of property. He lies and steals simply because lying and stealing are the obvious things for him to do. He does not think of doing anything else. The manner in which the story is told is characteristic, and should open the eyes of sentimentalists as to the real attitude of habitual criminals. Never, from first to last, is there an expression of genuine shame or the least contrition. There are, it is true, occasional sentences in which the man calls himself a fool, and betrays a glimmering of appreciation of the general want of sense and wisdom in his course, but there is no ring of sincere repentance nor of sorrow over a wasted life. This extraordinary character is simply of the opinion that he has not been clever enough. He never suspects that he has not been good enough to live a normal life among normal people. The truth is, he had no clear ideas of right and wrong.

Released from prison, and glad to be free, he always declared that now he was determined to "keep out of trouble." With him "trouble" meant "prison," and nothing else. Inevitably, surely, certainly, he was drawn into ways of crime. As water seeks its level, so he gravitated towards "trouble." To plan and execute an enterprise of robbery was the form of activity most natural to him. He was hindered by no scruples, schooled by no experience, tormented by no necessity. When arrested, and not before, he considered that he was "in trouble." He fretted over his punishment, but not over his offence.And yet this was a human being, one not without good traits. He was not, physically, a coward; on the contrary, he was simply and naturally fearless. He was kind of heart, gentle to children, and tender to animals. Under discipline, he was patient and obedient, a model prisoner, the wardens say. What he could not do was to stand alone and be a man in the world.Looking outward, this man was a shrewd and appreciative observer. His descriptions of natural scenes are vivid. There are few better stories of the life of a prisoner of war than his, and his characterizations of men and events are singularly apt. His eyes looked on the seamy side of life, and saw with clearness when fixed on any one or anything but himself. The conditions under which common sailors live have rarely been more vividly described. One can only wonder, while reading his plain story, told without heat or passion, how any man could follow such a life as he describes.

The work is without precedent in character. It is fascinating as a life story and as a study of human nature. It is a contribution to unconscious literature.

STANLEY WATERLOO.

CHAPTER I
MY FIRST VOYAGE

ON my mother's side I am of an old New York family. My great-grandfather served as colonel in the war of 1812. My father was born in Dublin, being a younger son of an Irish gentleman. He was educated to be a druggist, his father paying a large bonus to have him apprenticed to a celebrated firm in that business. His elder brother was ordained as a clergyman in the Church of England, and is now a high dignitary in the Church, if living. At the age of twenty, my father came to New York and started in business. My mother, then about fourteen or fifteen years old, became acquainted with him, and they were shortly afterward married, the match being a runaway one. I was born when mother was but sixteen years old. My parents lived comfortably; they sent me to boarding-schools at North Cornwall, Conn., Ballston Spa, N. Y., and the Military School at Danbury, Conn., and finally to one of the New York colleges. At that time I was very desirous to be a sailor, and have been sorry for it ever since. My parents objected, but afterwards consented. My father had many customers among the ship-owners and sea captains. At that time New York ship-owners had several vessels in the China trade, and sought to get well-taught American boys to educate them in seamanship and navigation, the idea being to make them officers of their ships as soon as they became competent. Seven boys were selected, I being one of them.

Father furnished me with a complete outfit for sea, and a set of navigation instruments and books. One thing I thought lacking—that was a pipe and tobacco. The sea-chest was sent to father's store. My younger brother, Charlie, was anxious to know what sailors wore at sea, so he examined the contents of the chest, and found a paper of cheap tobacco and a two-cent pipe.

Charles—"Oh, father, George smokes!"

Father—"Why, George, do you use tobacco?"

George—"No, father, I never have done so yet; but I always hear that sailors smoke at sea."

Father—"Well, George, throw that stuff away and come with me."

He then took me to a cigar-store, and bought me twelve half-pound papers of fine Turkish tobacco, some pipes, and a box containing one hundred fine cigars. What was the result? I never used a pipeful of that tobacco, nor a cigar, and not until years afterward, when I was forty-eight years old and in Joliet Prison, did I acquire the tobacco habit, first by chewing it and then by smoking pipes made out of tool handles on holidays—our only opportunity in that "hell-hole."

My father's friends had a full-rigged ship ready for sea at that time; there were the captain, first, second, and third mates, and a crew of about sixteen men of all nationalities. We seven boys were shipped on board as apprentices, at the rate of four dollars a month. The voyage was to be to Batavia, Island of Java, for a part cargo of coffee; from there to Shanghai, China, for the balance of the cargo, the new crop of tea, which would be ready for us by the time of our arrival.

The ship—we'll call her the Prospero—was to go out in ballast, as they had no cargo to send out. Three passengers were to go with us—a man, his sister, and her child. The sister was the wife of a pilot and opium smuggler in the Chinese waters. Ten kegs, containing five thousand Mexican dollars each, were also sent on board to be delivered to the branch firm in China. The fifty thousand dollars were placed in the male passengers' state-room, under his berth.

The ship was moved out from the dock, and anchored in the East River. Next morning, early, a large tugboat came alongside the ship. On board the tugboat was a large party, invited by the firm to have a pleasure trip while towing the ship out to sea. My father and mother were with the party, many of their friends, the captain's wife, and our passengers' friends among the number. It was a merry party. We weighed anchor. They gave us three cheers, and, wishing us a happy voyage, turned back for New York. We had commenced our voyage to the Indian Ocean.

No one had any idea how abruptly that voyage was to end, nor of the misery that was to follow. In less than two months this despatch was sent all over the country:

"CHARLESTON, S. C., *August, 1856.*

"The ship Prospero has arrived here, its captain having been murdered at sea. The first mate and two boys are under arrest by the United States officers, accused of having committed the murder."[A]

[A] Our passengers took passage from Charleston in another ship for China. They never reached their destination. The vessel caught fire at sea and all aboard perished. Not a soul was ever heard from.

Now comes the story of the mysterious murder. It has never been solved to this day, although many years have passed since it occurred.

The ship had been headed to the south-east, so as to get into the trade-winds near the coast of Africa. When near the Cape Verde Islands the captain was found dead in his bed, having been killed by being struck in the head with a ship's axe, having his throat cut, and being stabbed in the heart several times with a double-edged knife. The cabin steward went into the captain's state-room at eight o'clock to wake him for breakfast, and at once notified the first mate of the murder. The mate first went to the state-room, and then came on deck and ordered all the crew into the state-room. This is what we saw: the captain dead in bed, the only clothing on him being an undershirt, while the blood had stained all the bedding, had spurted up on the partitions around the berth for three or four feet, and also on the floor. Beside the body lay a small axe and a white handkerchief stained with blood, marked in one corner with the letter "L" embroidered in red silk, which letter had been partly picked out with a pen or knife, but was still discernible. The mate then informed us that he was acting captain of the ship. In our presence he wound up the two chronometers, which are always kept in the captain's room, for on them are dependent the daily calculations of the correct longitude.

We were finally ordered upon deck. The crew conversed together, and agreed among themselves that the ship should return to New York. The mate insisted upon continuing the voyage, and also asked the crew if they would allow him to place anyone under arrest whom he believed to be the murderer. They assented, and he ordered Henry Leroy to be put in irons.

The boy Leroy's hands were put behind his back, and he was handcuffed, then rusty iron chains were fastened to them and around his ankles. He was placed in the second mate's cabin on deck and the door was locked.

He was kept there until we reached Charleston. The weather was extremely warm. When taken out, he was completely covered with iron rust, which had stuck to his body with the perspiration, and he was not allowed to wash himself.

Shortly after Leroy was put in irons, he called for the second mate, and had a long conversation with him. The result was that I was handcuffed, hands behind my back, was taken on the quarter-deck, made to sit down with my back to a stanchion, and lashed to it by the passing of a rope several times around my body and once around my neck. I remained in that position for forty-eight hours, and was then put into the first mate's cabin with my hands fastened behind my back.

The mate still insisted on continuing the voyage, the crew upon returning. Then he proposed going back to Fayal, Western Islands, and leaving Leroy and me there, to be sent to New York by the American Consul, for trial. The crew would not agree to that. Nothing would satisfy them but to return home. So the ship was put about and headed for New York. We never got there, but fetched up at Bulls Bay, about forty miles north of Charleston, S. C.

The ship was anchored close to shore and the sails furled. Shortly afterward a steamer was sighted coming down the coast. Signals of distress were hoisted, and the steamer headed for us. The mate had one of our boats lowered, and, with a boat's crew of four men, went aboard the steamer. He wished to go to Charleston himself for a tugboat, also to telegraph to New York, but the men with him would not let him go, so he sent an order to Charleston for a tug, and a letter to the captain of the revenue cutter, explaining the situation.

The knife was never found; no blood stains could be found on any clothing or person aboard the ship. The axe had always hung in brackets over the captain's bed, that being the only trace that was left. The man who did the deed must have been covered with blood. No noise had been heard, although a number of persons were sleeping close by, and one half of the crew were awake and on duty continually. The corpse was placed in a water-cask, which was filled with brine and salt from the beef barrels. After the inquest, it was shipped to New York for burial. Next will be related the evidence against Leroy and myself.

Henry Leroy was born in Poughkeepsie, N. Y., his parents being quite wealthy. The elder brother was lieutenant commander in the U.S. Navy during the War of the Rebellion. Henry was the "black sheep" of the family, and was sent to sea in order to tame him down. The captain was instructed to be severe with him. He was very flighty, had a wild look in his eyes, and was very quarrelsome. In less than three weeks he had had four fights with the boys, the last one with me. There being no cargo on board, the boys had quarters fixed up for them between decks. Henry was in one watch and I in the other.

One night, at twelve o'clock, Henry came below and I was to go on watch. It was then we had the fight. There being only a thin partition between our place and the cabin, the noise woke the captain. The next morning the captain tied Henry to a dry-goods box and gave him a severe flogging with a rope's end. Henry afterward told some of the crew that he would be revenged for that flogging; that was the evidence against him.

Now for myself: All the boys would tell Henry all kinds of nonsense and he would believe it. I at one time proposed to him that we should kill everybody on board the ship; that we two should sail the ship to the coast of Africa, take the fifty thousand dollars in silver (weighing over four thousand pounds) and go home with it. Much to my surprise, he was willing to do so. Two or three times afterwards I amused myself with that yarn. That story, with some additions of his own, was the evidence against me. Some of his schoolmates afterwards stated under oath that it was impossible for him to tell the truth. A tugboat was sent to Charleston, and the ship was towed to that port. The United States Marshal came on board, and Henry and I were taken up to the city in the revenue cutter and put in the police station until the inquest was held. In a couple of days after our arrival the inquest was held on board the ship. Leroy and I were present. The captain's body was laid on deck and we were made to stand near it and look at the terrible sight while some of the jurors felt of our pulses, to see if we were unusually excited. Leroy testified that I had confessed to the murder at twelve o'clock the night it occurred, and that I had told him of it when the watches were changed. At my trial it was proved that I had not spoken to him from the evening before the murder until we were on the revenue cutter.

The coroner's jury ordered that we three be held for trial. So the mate was handcuffed and the three of us were taken to the Charleston jail, where we remained for about six months. As soon as the news reached New York, my father and Leroy's brother got letters of introduction to the most prominent men in Charleston and started for that city. In the meantime we had our examination before the United States Court Commissioner and were held over to the Federal grand jury without bail. The ship's crew were detained in jail as witnesses. It was a picnic for them, as they were each to receive one dollar and a half a day, comfortable quarters, the freedom of a large yard for exercise, and their food, with no work. On the ship it was hard labour with only twelve dollars a month for the voyage.

When my father and Mr. Leroy arrived they were welcomed by some of the leading citizens, and in a short time made many friends. They at once retained the four best lawyers in the city. We three prisoners were kept separate, but, as Henry and myself boarded with the jailer's family, we were together at meal hours. I made many friends, while Henry seemed to be disliked by everybody. The mate was kept in a cell by himself all the time. A leading Freemason came from New York to Charleston and retained a competent law firm for his defence. The Freemasons were the only friends he had, and they stood by him well.

No indictment was found against Leroy by the grand jury. He was released and put under bonds as a witness.

My trial came first. It lasted nearly a month and created much excitement North and South. Leroy's testimony was all there was against me. In the cross-examination he was badly rattled, and told so many lies that everybody got disgusted with him. He was proved to be a liar by some of his old schoolmates. The jury acquitted me without leaving their seats. They all shook hands with me, and I was congratulated by everybody. I was put under bonds as a witness.

The first mate's trial then took place. Circumstances looked bad for him. His cruelty to Leroy and myself made a bad impression on the jury. When I showed how I had been tied with ropes for two days, with my hands fastened behind my back for seventeen nights and days in the roasting hot weather, it actually made some of the jury grit their teeth. The jury retired, and were out quite a number of hours. Finally, they brought in a verdict of "Not guilty," but for a long time they stood ten for guilty and two for acquittal. After that, he never could get a mate's position on any ship in the United States, so he went to Australia and, when last heard from, was captain of an English ship.

The Prospero, on one of her voyages, was dismasted by a typhoon in the China Sea, was towed into one of the treaty ports in China and used as a coal hulk.

I went back to New York with father and mother, was gladly received by all my friends, and remained there until I took a notion in my thick head to go on a whaling voyage to the Pacific Ocean.

CHAPTER II
WHALING IN THE SOUTH PACIFIC

I WAS in the habit of walking around the docks of the East and North Rivers in New York and looking at the shipping. Fronting the river were a number of shipping offices for sailors, and some of them had a placard offering eighty dollars advance for men for the whaling service. So, one day, I went into one of the offices and stated my desires. I was very cordially received. That evening, with several others, I was sent to New Bedford, Mass. On our arrival there we were assigned to a sailors' boarding-house. In about two weeks afterward I was shipped on board the Courier, for a three years' cruise in the South Pacific Ocean, for the capture of sperm whales. I was to get one barrel of oil for myself out of every one hundred and ninety that we should capture. Sperm oil was worth about two dollars a gallon. No petroleum had been discovered at that time.

I was furnished with a seaman's outfit, which, with my board bill and expenses, amounted exactly to eighty dollars; that was the advance. I signed an agreement that the captain should pay that amount out of the first money due me. Captain Coffin, four mates, and four boat-steerers were the officers of the ship, with twenty-eight men before the mast, a cooper, blacksmith, carpenter, cook, and steward—forty-two men on the vessel, and the captain's wife and little boy.

The night before we sailed I wrote to my father and mother and let them know what I had done. I thought at the time that I knew more than they did. Well, the older I grow, the more I realize what a fool I have been all my life, and never a greater one than I am now at the age of sixty-two.

One morning early we weighed anchor, and were soon out of sight of land; then the voyage began in earnest. Much to my surprise, we had to take turns perched up aloft for two hours at a time on the top-gallant cross-trees, looking out for whales. Why, I never thought there was a whale within five thousand miles of New Bedford at that time, but I was mistaken. They are sometimes captured in sight of the harbour. The boat-steerers were kept busy fixing up their harpoons and lances, getting the boats ready, coiling the lines in the tubs etc. In the meantime the mates were watching the crew very closely to see which men were the most active.

After we were at sea about ten days all hands were called aft to the mizzen-mast. Then the mates, each in turn, picked out one man for his own boat's crew. Being light and active, I was made stroke-oarsman of the first mate's boat, and a lively job it proved to be, too. Soon we got in the warm latitudes and calm days, and then the boats would be lowered in order to give the crews exercise and practice in rowing. It was hard work, but we soon became expert oarsmen.

One day we sighted the Cape Verde Islands, and sailed among them for a few days. Boats were sent ashore; rotten tobacco—outfit quality—was traded to the natives for fruit; then I got in my work, so far as the fruit went. The ship then steered for the Island of Martinbas-Trinidado, 21° south latitude, for the purpose of ascertaining whether our chronometers were still correct, by comparing our observations with the longitude of the island, as that is known to a certainty.

Trinity Rock, as it is called also, is uninhabited, quite barren, and only a few miles in circumference. That is the place where we had our first adventure. The first mate's boat was to take the crew, with the captain, his wife and child, also three old muskets and ammunition, and land them in a seaman-like manner on the island. The boat's party with the old army muskets were to kill a number of mythical goats on land.

We pulled close to the shore, just outside of the heavy surf, trying to find a safe place to land. Finally we came to an opening in the reef. Inside, the water looked smooth and inviting, and there was also a nice sandy beach. To the left of the reef was the wreck of a French ship, the bowsprit pointing straight up into the air. While looking at the wreck, we saw a large green turtle just ahead of the boat. Then visions of turtle soup with our goat's meat dawned upon us. It chanced, though, that in trying to capture that turtle we made a great mistake, for just at that time a very-heavy surf came over the reef and capsized our boat. Things were badly mixed for a time. Boat, oars, men, and the captain's wife and child were going in every direction. Finally things quieted down a little, and we landed on the beach. We got the boat and what oars we could, and then took a rest on the burning hot sand. The weather being very warm, the boat's crew all wore leather slippers and no stockings. We had to run up and down on the sand with our bare feet, as the aforesaid slippers were lost when the boat went over. I picked hard little short thorns out of my feet for days afterward. They came from dried-up vines that grew in the sand.

The beach was honeycombed with large holes, and each hole contained a big yellow land-crab. Every step we took, snap would go a big pair of claws for our feet. We had also lost our straw hats, so we had the full benefit of the sun on our bare heads. A number of wild land birds of a good, healthy size would swoop down upon us. It was anything but a pleasure at that time, and the muskets being lost also, the captain and mate changed their minds about the goat business.

The cause of our disaster was made clear to us in a short time. The surf for about ten minutes would run low, and then would be followed by three tremendous rollers in succession. It was the latter that wrecked us on a barren island. We soon got tired of life on shore. The question was how to get away.

In the meantime, while we were on the goat expedition, the second mate's boat had left the ship on a fishing excursion. They anchored the boat near shore, outside the surf, and were hauling the fish in at a lively rate. We needed their assistance. As the mate still had his shoes on his feet, he went quite a distance down the beach and made signals for the boat to follow him back. When they got opposite to us we explained the situation. By watching for a good chance, they pulled in quickly and threw us the end of a harpoon-line, and got outside of the reef. We fastened the line to the bow of our boat, and when a low surf came in launched it, were towed out by the other boat, and arrived on board the ship very much disgusted with the whole business.

The old Courier's yards were braced around and we were off for Cape Horn, 56° south latitude. One day, it being quite calm, the lookouts at the mast-head noticed a lot of sea-gulls flying around in a circle, and under them something floating in the water. We thought it might be a dead whale, so the mate's boat was lowered. We found it to be an old cask, which must have been in the water for years, as it was thickly covered with barnacles.

We towed the cask to the ship and hoisted it on board. As it came out of the sea we noticed that the staves were completely honeycombed by the sea-worms. The water was spurting out as if it were a sprinkling-pot. We had just got it over the ship's rail when it burst, and the contents fell on the deck. It proved to be palm-oil, probably from some vessel in the African trade that had been wrecked. It had, no doubt, drifted many thousands of miles. We saved two barrels of oil out of our catch.

The weather soon began to get much cooler, and storms were frequent; then we began to see the albatross and Cape Horn pigeons. The latter is about the size of a domestic pigeon, but has webbed feet and a hooked bill, and is the only wild bird having variegated plumage, no two being marked alike. We caught quite a number of the albatross, some measuring seventeen feet from tip to tip of wing. We caught them with large fishhooks baited with a big piece of salt pork. The bait would float on the surface of the water. We had them walking all over the decks, as they cannot fly unless they run on water to give them a good start. The large webbed feet make excellent money pouches when dried and properly dressed.

In the month of January, midsummer in the southern hemisphere, we sighted Staten Land, the extreme southern point of South America, and ordinarily designated as Cape Horn. For the first time we then saw the Pacific Ocean, "so near and yet so far," for just at this time we were struck by a heavy northwest gale. A close-reefed main top-sail and storm stay-sail was all we could carry with the ship headed as close to the wind as possible, so as to ride over the mountain-like waves. The helm was lashed hard down, as there was no steerage way.

There we were, drifting to the south for about three weeks before the gale broke, and we were able to make sail on the ship. It was daylight for twenty-two hours, and the other two hours of the twenty-four could not be called dark. Such days would be delightful for farmers in this part of the world. Soon after the storm we got fair winds, and were on our cruising grounds off the southern coast of Chile and northern part of Patagonia (the new boundary gives the whole coast to Chile now).

The ship's crew was then divided into four watches, with a boat-steerer in charge and only one watch on duty at a time, so we had plenty of leisure. Every night, all sail but two would be close reefed, top-sails would be furled, then the ship would be headed offshore until midnight, and would then go about and stand inshore until daylight, when all sail would be set again. At certain seasons whales come down the coast going south, and we were keeping a bright lookout for them.

Each whaleboat's outfit consists of three harpoons, two lances, one cutting-in spade, one tub with three hundred fathoms of five-eighths'-inch whale-line, one extra tub with one hundred fathoms, one tight keg containing boat compass, lantern, steel and flint, and some sea biscuit. The latter articles are used only in case the boat is lost from the ship, which frequently happens.

There is a number of different species among the whales. They are all mammals, bringing forth and suckling their calves. On attacking a cow and calf together, it is the custom to kill the latter first, as the cow will never desert her calf. The sulphur-bottom whale is the largest, but it is never harpooned, as it is too dangerous, and will always run all the line out of the tubs before it stops sounding. The sperm whale furnishes the most valuable oil. The sperm whale throws its flukes, or tail, up and down when attacked, so it is possible for a boat to approach one head, or fluke, on. The right whale furnishes the common oil, and in larger quantities; sometimes one fish will yield two hundred and fifty barrels of oil, as well as many pounds of whalebone, now very scarce and valuable. It hangs in large thin sheets from the jaws, wide at the top, and tapering to a narrow point with hair-like fringe on the edges. The right whale can be attacked only "head on," as they throw their flukes from side to side. They are captured in the cold northern seas, the sperm in southern waters. One hundred barrels is a large yield from one fish of the latter species.

We saw several whales, but could not get near them. Finally, one big fellow was sighted, and all boats were lowered, the first mate's being in the water first. Having a good fair wind, we set the boat's sail. In a short time we were close to the whale. Being stroke-oarsman, it was my duty to keep the sheet of the sail in my hand, having one turn around a cleat. The boat-steerer stands up with a harpoon ready. Soon we were right on top of the fish, the sheet was "let go," a harpoon was thrown just as we were going over the whale's back, and then the fun began. The line leads from the tub to a post in the stern of the boat—two turns around it—and thence through a cleat in the boat's bows. The tub was alongside me. I was kept busy throwing water on the line, so that the friction would not set fire to the post, or "loggerhead." The mate was holding that rope in his hand all the time, just keeping all the strain on it possible without sinking the boat. If he had let a kink get into that line as it came from the tub, the boat and crew would have gone under water in quick order. If he had let the line slip off the "loggerhead" it would probably have killed every man in the boat. The noise and sawing of that rope, with the smoke and steam from the "loggerhead," I can remember to this day. The whale stopped sounding at last. We were watching which way the line would point as the whale was coming up, and discovering that the line was directly under us, we got away from that spot in a very lively manner, as that was a sure sign that his whaleship intended to have a fight with the boat. They frequently play that trick, and the crew have to jump into the water, provided they have a chance to do so. In a few minutes our friend came to the surface, spouted water, and then started off "dead to windward"—they invariably do so—at a terrific speed. The boat-steerer and mate now changed places, and all the men except myself reversed positions, so as to face the boat's bow. They hauled in the line, and I coiled it carefully back in the tub. When alongside of the whale, the mate threw a lance as often as possible, aiming at a point just behind the fin, at what is called the "life." It is a mass of very large veins just under the backbone, that is used by the whale as a reservoir for the extra blood which it requires while under water. When that is once cut, a whale spouts blood instead of water. Down he went again. We had to keep up that sort of work for about two hours, until finally the blood was thrown from the spout, and we were completely covered with it. In a little while our capture began to swim in a circle and on one side with one fin out of water, and soon he was dead. Sharks made their appearance in the water so close to the boat that we could strike them with our oars, and hundreds of large sea-birds were wildly flying around us, all attracted by the blood. In the meantime the other boats had been rowing hard to overtake us if possible and assist, or pick us up, in case of accident. As we were dead to windward, and several miles from the ship, all the boats had to fasten on and tow the whale back, and a big contract it was.

On the ship everything had been made ready for "cutting-in." The fish was fastened alongside by heavy iron chains and, with heavy tackles from the main masthead and loading to the windlass, the blubber was slowly hoisted on deck. The captain and the mate did the cutting with long-handled blubber spades. They kept cutting one continuous strip two feet wide, and at every eight feet would cut a hole and hook in the next tackle; and so they kept on hoisting and lowering until the blubber was all on board. It was a process similar to peeling an orange. The strain from the windlass kept the whale's body revolving in the water as the blubber was cut. The head was cut off and hoisted on deck entire. The chains being removed, the carcass, weighing many tons, sank to the bottom, the sharks voraciously following it.

Then a fire was built under the try-pots, with wood. As the oil was boiled from the blubber it would be put in a cooling-pot and thence into casks, the scraps being used for fuel. That work lasted for about a week, everybody working hard. It was nothing but oil all over the ship—clothing, food, and water—all had a liberal allowance. Eighty barrels was the total of that catch. A few weeks later we sighted a school of young whales. Several other ships being close at the time, it was boats, whales, sharks, and everything mixed up.

Our boatswain got knocked overboard while we were fast to a whale; another boat picked him up. We got only two whales out of the lot, fifteen barrels of oil out of one and twenty out of the other. Some of the other ships got five and six. About that time the season on that coast ended. The captain concluded to make for port and get fresh provisions and water, and then make a trip north of the equator. The water in our casks was getting rather stale; it tasted and smelled like a strong decoction of dead rats. San Carlos, Chiloe Island, was the port we anchored in. I took a look at the shore and made up my mind that if I ever got my feet on dry land they would stay there.

CHAPTER III
A SAILOR ASHORE

THE water casks were hoisted up from the hold, lowered overboard and towed ashore, to be filled with fresh water. In about a week's time we finished that job, then all hands were to have twenty-four hours' liberty on shore—eight men at a time. My name was one of the first to be called. We received two dollars cash for spending money. Taking my chum aside, I quietly bid him good-bye, and then got into the boat. Everything was strange to me on shore—the customs, language, and sights. I got acquainted with a young American from another ship, by the name of Amos, and learned that he also was desirous to quit the oil business. During the day we kept with the other sailors, visiting the dance-houses. When evening came we both struck out for the woods.

The natives were very kind to us, knowing that we were runaway sailors. They would invite us to sleep in their houses during the nights, when they would teach us to talk Spanish. It must have been very amusing to them, as they were continually laughing and saying "Bueno" (good). In the daytime we would go down to the beach to see whether our ships had left harbour yet. In about three weeks' time we had the pleasure of seeing both vessels standing out to sea. It was the last time that I saw the Courier on that coast. Her old ribs now lie in the sands at the mouth of Charleston Harbour, South Carolina. During the war the Government purchased a number of condemned whalers and fitted them up for sea, when they were loaded with stone and taken to Charleston Harbour, dismantled, and sunk in the channels, in order to blockade the harbour more effectually. The whole world made a fuss about it. That blockading experiment was a dismal failure, as it was only a short time until the waters of the Ashley and Cooper rivers, combined with the ocean currents, washed out much deeper and better channels. I saw the ship just before she was sunk and bade the old Courier a last farewell.

A few days after our ships had left San Carlos we walked into town, interviewed the captain of the port, and asked for our discharge, saying that our ships had gone to sea and abandoned us in a foreign port. Well, we got our papers all right. We needed them at that time, as nobody could go from one town to another without having documents to show who they were— not even the natives. The country is under strict military government, the army having control of everything. My friend and I finally came to the conclusion that we were in a bad fix, being in a foreign country, not able to speak the language, and having no money. There was no work to be obtained. After a while we made up our minds to work our passage to Valparaiso on some merchant vessel. We remained around the landing-dock for several days. Every captain we spoke to replied to us kindly, but they had no places for us. In the meantime we had taken trips to the beach, digging clams to eat. The people in the town were not so liberal to us as were the natives who lived at a distance.

While loafing around the dock one day we got into conversation with an American, a runaway whaler. He told us that he was a carpenter, had been living several years in the country, and was married to a young Chilean woman. He wanted Amos to go to another of the islands and work with him. My friend would not go without me, so Tom, the carpenter, proposed that I should also go, as there was a blacksmith by the name of Bill who would be glad to have me as a helper. Now was the formation of a fine quartette of Yankees begun! Amos was a graduate of a Down East reform school, very handy with tools, a fine-looking young fellow, but he could not read nor write, and he never could learn the Spanish language; reference to a terribly ugly temper and vicious disposition completes his description. Our new friend took us to his house, gave us an introduction to his wife, a very pretty young woman about sixteen years old. (They marry as young as eleven and twelve years of age.)

Manuela was not educated and was exceedingly lazy, with lax ideas as to morality and virtue. Tom informed us that the next morning we would start for the Island of Calabucco, as he had house rent free there and a contract to lengthen a boat for a priest. During the night Amos got out of bed, went to another house, and stole the only double-barrelled shotgun in that town. Tom hid it in a mattress. After breakfast, we carried what household goods there were down to the dock. A tool-chest, a couple of pots, some dishes, a few clothes, and the bedding completed the outfit.

Everything was put on board a sloop, and then we started for our new home. During the trip Señora Manuela was watching my friend Amos; the result was that Tom told me that I should live with him, and Amos would have to go to Bill's house. On our arrival we soon had our house in order. Opposite to our place was the residence of the priest. I saw a number of dirty children—about eight—running about the place, also a woman. As I got better acquainted I had every reason to believe that poverty, piety, and celibacy were omitted from the Father's creed.

After a rest of several days, we went to his reverence's yard and had a look at the boat. It was an old yawl from some ship, very short and broad. We were to make it three feet longer by piecing it in the centre. The boss asked me for my advice. I knew a lot about boats then. Oh, yes; a very easy job— if we only knew how! We waited a few days longer before going to work.

Money was very scarce in that town, so they used a small cedar-board for currency. The size was about six feet long, six inches wide, and half an inch thick. The value of each was about six cents. The stores were small, and, for that reason, the cedar-boards were piled up in the back yards until some merchant would buy them at the market price—seven dollars a hundred—and ship them to Valparaiso. There were no lights in the streets at night-time, and the night watchman would call out the hours and half-hours and the state of the weather during the whole night, so that one could always know exactly his whereabouts. My friend Amos, with his past experience, took advantage of that fact, and induced me to go into the lumber business with him. Night after night we were busy climbing over fences and carrying off cedar-boards. About thirty-five each was considered a fair load for a trip. In the daytime we took them to different places and made our purchases.

One day we at Tom's house got excited. The double-barrelled shotgun was gone. We watched our chance and stole it back from the house presided over by Bill and Amos; however, they stole it back again in course of time, and kept it. Tom's ranch did not suit me, so I went to work for a native shoemaker. Amos quit Bill and went to Tom. I quit the shoemaker and went with Bill. About that time Tom concluded it would be easier to make a new boat out and out. The padre was of the same opinion. He told Tom he could have the old boat for his own use. So the job began in earnest, but our friend was not a very good man for that kind of work; he could not do anything until he took the old yawl apart for patterns to work by. It was about one year before the new boat was finished. In the town was a man who owned a launch—a home-made affair, with planks two and a half inches thick. For oars he had rough, heavy poles with pieces of boards fastened on the ends for blades. Nothing but a boat-race would settle the point as to which was the faster. Our padre was quite a sport. At any cock-fighting, gambling, horse- or boat-racing he was always the umpire and prime mover. Eight sheep and one barrel of cider were the stakes to be raced for. One Sunday morning, just after mass, the race took place. The padre's boat came in about a half mile ahead—the whole course was not two miles. Tom's reputation as a boat-builder was away up in consequence, and he got the "big-head" badly. That night he gave a select party at his house in honour of the event. Aguardiente was the only refreshment served; and towards midnight all were drunk, Tom especially so. A thin partition separated the bedroom from the main apartment. Our host, in staggering around, fell against the door, and tumbled on to his own bed, only to find it already occupied. Then there was a row; the guest jumped out of the window, with the other occupant a close second.

My new employer, the blacksmith, was a fine-looking man of six feet two inches in height, and built in proportion. He had a fair complexion and light hair hanging in ringlets down his shoulders. He was from Baltimore, Md. Swearing, drinking aguardiente, and talk—that was all he was good for. His wife was a widow seventeen years of age when he married her. They had three little boys, the most vicious little wretches that I ever came in contact with. As for their home, it was squalid and filthy. No floor, and the fire was in the centre of the only room. On each side was a board resting on stone: that was the only place we had to sit down. A most cheerful family circle we made. The children were continually raising Cain, and Bill swearing at them in Spanish. As yet none of the bosses had ever said anything about wages. However, I never had any work to do, so that equalized affairs.

One day Bill—or Guillermo, as he was called—was wanted at a saw-mill on the mainland. A freshet had made a wreck of the mill and dam. None of the natives was willing to work, so Bill induced Amos and me to go with him. At last I was working for fifty cents a day. After a while we got the dam repaired, and then fixed up the mill. It then dawned upon Don Fernando's mind that he had no one to run the aforesaid mill. So he made a contract with us to do the sawing at two cents a board, we to "find" ourselves in food and cooking utensils. Bill sent for his family; Amos and I occupied a small room in the mill for a living apartment, where we were to keep bachelors' hall. Our stock of provisions was furnished on credit from the employer's store. Wheat flour was worth eight cents a pound, but wheat was worth only fifty cents a bushel. This seeming profit was used up in sending the wheat to Valparaiso for grinding and then having it shipped back as flour, as no railroads were there then.

The mill was a most primitive affair; the amount of labour was astounding, the results of our toil much more so; a hundred boards was our largest day's work, and I will guarantee that not any two of them were of equal thickness at the end. Some days we would have no logs to saw; other days there would be no water in the dam. Bill had one cent as foreman, Amos and I each half a cent a board. Our average was about twenty cents a day each.

We found ourselves gradually getting into debt for provisions and clothing. After talking over our financial affairs one evening, we came to the conclusion that our prospects looked gloomy. About bedtime Amos put on his hat and coat and invited me to do the same. He was always sullen, so I never asked him any questions. When we were outside the room he informed me that in future he would live a —— sight cheaper and better than he had been doing in the past. All I could say was, "Amen, brother!" My friend proved to be a good forager; before morning we had a nicely dressed sheep hanging up in our room, also a big supply of potatoes under the bed. That was the only time in my life that I was guilty of sheep-stealing. We lived high on roast mutton and potatoes; but, alas! we were found out. They blamed Amos for the whole business; but, on attempting to arrest him, they made a mistake, as he pulled out a big knife, and coolly walked away from that part of the country. Afterward he stole a horse; that was the last we heard about him in Chile.

Every one called me "Bueno muchacho" (good boy), while Amos was designated "Muy picaro" (great rascal). Don Fernando Andrade was over sixty years of age; he had a fine-looking wife and quite a number of children—the oldest one twenty-six years, and the youngest six months old. He took quite an interest in me, as I was always very quiet, polite, and strictly temperate. Finally, he had me live with his own family, and treated me as if I were one of his own sons. They used to laugh and make fun of me because I washed my hands and face twice a day. In that part of the country they never wash themselves at all: "Se maltrata el cuero" (it ill-treats the skin) was their reason, I presume; laziness also. About that time I wrote to my father and mother in New York. The postage then on a foreign letter was fifty cents, with only one mail a month on that coast. In about four months I received an answer from San Francisco, Cal. My father had failed in business in New York, indorsing notes, and a panic ruined him. He was doing well in California, and wanted me to come there. Don Fernando had a contract for a large number of railroad-ties for Peru. The natives would cut and pile them on the beach ready for loading. A schooner was sent up from Don Carlos for a cargo of them. The captain was an Englishman, and we became quite friendly. He offered to take me to San Carlos whenever I wished to go. By the time the schooner was loaded I got homesick, and, all at once, I made up my mind to go home, so I bid Don Fernando good-bye. He was sorry to have me leave, but would not coax me to remain away from my parents.

CHAPTER IV
I TAKE TO THE SEA AGAIN

AT San Carlos was a large ship receiving the ties as they were brought from the different islands. The captain shipped me as an ordinary seaman at ten dollars a month. The vessel was the Androkolis, of Copenhagen, Denmark. Our destination was Callao, Peru. I never reached San Francisco, although I sailed eighteen hundred miles towards that city. San Carlos was 42° and Callao 12° south latitude. The crew of the Androkolis was composed of Danes, Swedes, Norwegians, two Hollanders, and one Englishman, every one of them speaking a different language from mine, except the man from Liverpool, Jimmy Kincaid by name. Now Jimmy and I became chums. He was very short and broad, and possessed unusually large hands and feet. He was about twenty years old. We little knew what hardships were in store for us when we became friends. If he is alive to-day, he remembers, beyond all doubt, the night we saw the Flying Dutchman while rounding Cape Horn on another vessel.[B] We both saw that vessel—of course it was only an illusion—but we were both badly scared for a few minutes, as certain death appeared imminent. I will explain it in time. There are a few thousand miles of sea to be sailed over before we come to the story of that night.

[B] Like the Wandering Jew on land, there is a ship at sea sailing on and on until doomsday, manned by a crew of very old Dutchmen, who are expiating some sin.

We had a very pleasant voyage. Sailing north towards the equator, the weather was gradually getting warmer. In about four weeks' time we sighted the Island of San Lorenzo, an immense, high rock which formed the western side of Callao Harbour. The ship's sails were taken in and furled, all but the top-sails. At last we came to anchor. Where our ship lay in the bay was directly over the old city. A number of years ago, during one night, an earthquake submerged Callao and raised up San Lorenzo from beneath the waters. Five miles inland is the city of Lima, the capital of Peru and the burial-place of Pizarro, the conqueror of that country. The only railroad on that coast at that time was the five-mile track connecting the two cities. Jimmy and I rowed the captain ashore in the ship's boat. Sitting on the steps when we arrived there was my old friend Amos. We were much surprised to meet again. He told me all about himself since leaving the saw-mill in Chile so abruptly. He invited me to visit him at the hospital, although there was nothing in his appearance to indicate that he was an invalid.

Lighters came to the ship, and the unloading of our cargo commenced. Jimmy and I were promoted to be cook and steward of the vessel, I being the latter. One Sunday we had an afternoon holiday on shore. The captain let us have only one dollar each out of the wages due to us. The first place we visited was the hospital, in quest of Amos. It was a terribly hot day. On a large grassy plain fronting the building were a number of healthy-looking men playing a very lively game of ball. You can imagine our surprise when Amos informed us that they were the patients belonging to the hospital. The explanation was simple enough. Every man aboard of an American ship has to pay twenty-five cents a month to support the marine hospitals. A ship cannot get clearance papers until it is paid. That entitles the sailors to admission to any marine hospital in the United States when they are taken sick. If in a foreign port, the American consul is obliged to pay for their keeping at whatever hospital may be found in that place. The consul for Callao was a kind-hearted old man by the name of Mills. Any American sailor who would go to him and say, "I am sick, Consul," would get an order for admission at once. A number of seamen imposed on him. It was an object for them to get their board and clothing free while they were waiting only for seamen's wages to rise as high as possible; then they would ship for some long voyage. The hospital authorities were easily enough satisfied, as they were well paid, and the patients were able to attend to their own ailments.

After our return to the ship, Jimmy was continually coaxing me to remain in Peru with him, and live among the natives for a while. I was anxious to get to San Francisco, but no ships in harbour were bound in that direction, although a number arrived from there, loading with guano and going around Cape Horn. At last I promised to go with Jimmy. He had eighty dollars due him, and I twelve, but the captain would not discharge us and pay us off. Then we got mad and determined to go anyway. We got our clothes packed up in bags, ready for any chance we could get to leave the ship. With the ship's telescope we took a good look at the shores of the bay. At one place the beach looked as if it would be a good landing-place for us; it appeared like the edge of a mill-pond. Our chance soon came. The boat had not been hoisted up out of the water, as was customary, but had been left overnight fastened to the ship's side. Each sailor in turn had to stand "anchor watch" during the night for one hour. He would then wake up his relief and go to bed. There was a Dutchman whose turn would be at three o'clock in the morning. I told him when he was called to awaken me, then he could go to sleep again, as Jimmy and I had to make fresh bread for breakfast, and we would do the anchor watching. Sure enough, "Dutchy" woke me up; then I called Jimmy, and in a short time we had our clothes in the boat, also a good double-barrelled shotgun, a pair of pistols, a silver watch, and a couple of dozen of clean shirts belonging to the captain. We wished to have something for the money that was due us.

Away we went for the landing-place that we had selected. It was dark, and quite difficult to see the beach; it appeared to us as though we were close to a wall, several feet high, of rocks. The noise of the surf also made us careful about landing. At last we discovered that it was low tide, and the wall was only the wet cobble-stones left uncovered at low water. We pulled hard, so as to run through the surf, and we went up the beach on a heavy roller. Jimmy stood in the bow of the boat, ready to jump and hold the rope, or "painter," as it is called, as the surf receded. He was a little slow in jumping, consequently the boat went back with the surf in a hurry, Jimmy's feet went from under him, and he landed head first on the rocks. The next roller brought the boat in again; this time we succeeded, and got everything on land. The boat was pushed out in the surf, and was found the next day floating bottom up. We heard afterward that it was reported we had both been drowned.

About nine o'clock I went to the hospital and told Amos what we had done. He agreed to introduce us to a friend of his, who would take care of us for a few days. That afternoon he brought a man with him to our camping-place. In the evening everything was taken to a house in the city. It very soon dawned upon us that we had got into the worst sailors' "robbers' roost" that was in the town. Our clothing and possessions were all locked up in a room. We were made to understand that to remain in the house would be the best thing we could do. From what I afterward saw in that place I had reason to believe they meant what they said. The Vigilance Committee in San Francisco had driven all the tough characters out of the city. Quite a number of the worst ones went to Callao and started sailor boarding-houses and saloons. They formed a "ring" for mutual benefit. The English consul and a number of the Peruvian port officers were in with them. A fine crowd of robbers they were. They kept the sailors' wages high, beyond doubt, but only for the reason that they would have more for themselves when they cheated the seamen out of two months' advance pay. It is always customary to give that much on long voyages, or "deep sea trips," as they call them. After a few days' sojourn in our quiet boarding-house, we concluded that any change would be for the better. The landlord informed us that a small English brig was going up the coast, and that he could ship us both as ordinary seamen. In the English merchant marine a man cannot be shipped unless he has a discharge from another vessel; in the American service no papers are needed. We obtained discharges belonging to other sailors, who had no use for them. The landlord took us to the English consul's office. My name was to be Michael Murray. The clerk read the law, as is customary; one rule especially—that any man assuming another name would forfeit all wages. We had given bogus papers. When I went to sign the articles I was rather embarrassed, as I had forgotten my new name, so they had to tell me what it was. We were taken to our new ship, which was anchored out in the bay.

I was not greatly pleased when I found what was in store for me. The wages were twenty-five dollars a month. The landlord had received fifty dollars—two months' pay—in advance. He was to deduct my board bill and give me the balance of the money, but I never got a cent of it. I had been "shanghaied," as the sailors call it. Instead of going up the coast, as I was told we were to do, I found we were bound for Cork, Ireland, a voyage of eighty-five hundred and twenty miles. The vessel itself was a "holy terror," very heavily rigged, while everything on board was old and played out, the rusty blocks, with heavy running gear, making it very hard work for us, especially as we had a crew of only six men, where twelve seamen, at least, should have been a crew for that old tub. The cargo was guano in bulk, as a scow would be loaded with dirt. Our sleeping quarters were in the forecastle, situated in the bow of the vessel. Everything was covered with guano. As we had to live below, it was our first object to clean up the place. Buckets of water were passed down the scuttle, and the place was cleaned up as well as we could do it; but it was of no use; the smell of ammonia made us sick. Some would vomit, others bled at the nose, and a thick black phlegm would form in our throats. The weather being warm, we slept on the deck, as we could not endure it in the forecastle below.

Guano is the droppings from sea-birds, which have been accumulating for thousands of years. The Chincha Islands, belonging to Peru, have an inexhaustible supply. No rain ever falls in that country, consequently nothing is washed away. The depth of the guano is from four to eight feet. When a ship is to be loaded with guano, it has to go to Callao first for a permit, then to the Chincha Islands. The cargo is put in by Chinese coolies, and then the vessel returns to Callao for a clearance, also to pay a certain amount per ton.

CHAPTER V
ON THE BRIG GRENFALLS

THE brig Grenfalls, of Sunderland, was our packet. Just before getting up anchor we asked the captain if he intended to get more men for the voyage. He curtly said "No." Then we came very near having a mutiny. Finally we agreed to get up the anchor, especially as the captain threatened to make a signal to the British man-of-war for assistance, so we had to go anyway. I remember seeing the United States frigate Merrimac in the harbour and wishing myself aboard her. The next time I saw that vessel it had been transformed into an ironclad by the rebels, and had destroyed the Congress and the Cumberland. The first week at sea we had very pleasant weather. After that it became gradually colder and stormy. No more sleeping on deck. The forecastle was the only place for us then.

Two quarts of water a day was our allowance, one pint each for breakfast, dinner, and supper; the remaining pint was for drinking during the following hours of the twenty-four. The hardtack that we had to eat was covered with green mould and full of large white meal worms. The salt pork was red with rust and filled with white spots. Probably the hogs were killed on account of measles and pickled for sailors' use at sea. The salt beef, or horse-meat, as it was called, was rather tough eating; besides, everything we ate or drank was highly flavoured with guano.

Off the coast of Patagonia we encountered a heavy northwest gale of wind; then our misery began in earnest. In harbour the deck was only sixteen inches above water; in rough weather the seas were continually washing over the decks. It was necessary to make gill guys by fastening ropes diagonally across the deck from forward to aft. In going from one place to another we could take hold of the guy nearest to us, then get over and reach for the next before letting go of the first one. That was the only way to keep from being washed overboard or thrown against the ship's rail.

One night we heard water swashing under the forecastle deck. We told the mate about it. There was a bulkhead dividing the forecastle from the main hold; on the other side was a short half-deck. We cut a hole in it and lowered a lantern. A lot of water could be plainly seen. The vessel rolling would mix the guano with it. By working all of the men we got it out. All the crew supposed it to be the same water that we used in cleaning out our quarters, but we said nothing about it to the mate. We used plenty of it and let it run into the hold. The next night we heard the same swashing again; then we knew there was a leak somewhere. From that time the muddy water had to be taken out in buckets and thrown on the deck twice a day. The seas would wash it overboard. The leak was found at last. A long iron bolt in the foremast rigging chains had become rusty and worked loose. The bolt went through one of the knees which supported the deck beams. Being below the loading line, the water would come in and drop on the guano. It could not drain through and get to the pumps.

All our clothing got very rotten; shoes and boots became very hard; any cuts or bruises on our bodies would not heal up; the palms of our hands were full of black holes the size of a pin-head; the skin became very thick, and would crack open at each finger-joint; our hair fell out, so that we became prematurely bald. The windlass also, every time the brig rolled, would slide a few inches from side to side, and would make the deck-seams open enough to allow the water to drop through on our beds. For three months our beds and clothing were dripping wet. When I went to bed I would get to sleep at once, and it was hard to wake me up. Going from a wet, steaming hot bed to stand watch on deck in that cold weather was no joke. Each watch changes every four hours. Jimmy and myself were in the mate's watch: two hours each at the wheel and two on the lookout. The officers were the worst cowards that I ever came in contact with at sea. At one time the captain did not come on deck for two weeks. There being no sun visible in that storm, no observations could be taken, so we had to sail by "dead reckoning." The mate would sneak into the cabin during most of the watch, and leave Jimmy and myself to take the chances of being washed overboard. When it was my lookout I would go to the cook's galley, and let the brig do her own watching. My chum did the same as I. Two hours at wheel-steering would knock a prize-fighter out. There was a very short iron tiller in the rudder-post. The wheel-chains were iron and slack; consequently, every time the rudder would jerk, the helmsman would be raised up a couple of feet, and then landed back again almost quick enough to snap his head off. I was thrown clear over the wheel several times. I tried the experiment of letting go a few times when the wheel commenced to gripe; then I did come to grief; it would whirl around one way and then back again. In trying to stop it, the spokes would hit me a good rap on the knuckles. One eighth of a point off the course is considered bad steering, but our old packet would "yaw" off five whole points each way in spite of us. It seemed as if the stern were trying to get ahead of the bow. Whenever I see a mule turning his head back to look at his driver, it always reminds me of the old brig Grenfalls. Besides the leak, a new danger confronted us.

As we neared Cape Horn the seas became much higher and the storm increased. The sun would rise at nearly ten o'clock in the morning, and go down at two in the afternoon. The clouds were very heavy, and seemingly close to the water. Heavy snow-storms were common. The wind, however, was in our favour. Sometimes there would be a lull in the gale; then more sail would have to be set to keep us ahead of the immense high waves, else one might come over our stern and sink us. On the other hand was the danger of going too fast; in that case the vessel would run under and, loaded as it was, must go down like a piece of iron. Another trouble was that we had to heave-to frequently, and that was very dangerous. Now going before the wind and then swinging around head to wind, as near as possible, compelled us to get into the trough of the sea. If we had been struck by one of those huge waves broadside on, the voyage would have terminated just then.

The gale that brought us to Cape Horn followed the Pacific coast to Staten Island, and then up the Atlantic Ocean. One day, as we were sailing too slowly, a great wave almost broke over our stern. The main top-gallant-sail was set in a hurry. A few hours afterward the wind increased, and the light sail had to be taken in. Before Jimmy and I could get aloft to furl it, there was nothing left. The wind had blown it away in small pieces. That night we were compelled to heave to again. No matter which way the tub's head was pointed, we were going in the right direction, even if it were stern first, drifting before the wind. Our cook and steward was a wild, red-headed fellow—Darwin's missing link. My chum accused him of cheating us out of our pint of drinking water. They were quarrelling all day about it. That night Reddy came to the forecastle scuttle while I was getting some hard-tack ready for eating—that is, hunting for meal worms. Reddy commenced the row again. He was just going to paralyze Jimmy! I had not said a word yet, but my chum was not going to be hurt if I could help it. At last the man became quite brave. He told Jimmy he'd lick him and his chum together. The chum was myself. So we invited him to come below. He lost no time in doing so. Before he got half-way down we jumped for him. What a good thrashing he got for his trouble! When we got through pounding him, he was dragged to the opening in the bulkhead. Our intention was to throw him down the hole into the water and the guano. We pushed too hard, so that he went a-flying over the right place, very luckily, as he would have been smothered in the guano-water. Reddy stayed in bed for two days. He told the captain that the whole crew had tried to kill him. When he got out of bed his face was blue, green, and yellow; this, with the eyes nicely blacked and his red hair, made a fine combination of colours. Neither one of us had been struck once, and there was no more trouble about water.

One night, just after being relieved from watch, all hands were called to shorten sail. On deck I had to go again. There we were kept for thirty-two hours, tending to the sails and bailing out water and guano. A few nights afterward I was at the wheel. The mate sneaked into the cabin; Jimmy was in the galley. There I was, tired out, my clothes dripping wet with sea water and the wheel nearly jerking my arms off. Suddenly the brig yawed off and was struck by a heavy sea. I could feel the vessel quivering under my feet; with one hand I could not move the wheel either way. I thought we were sinking and that my day had come. The water on deck was above my knees. Suddenly the wheel began its old tricks again, very much to my relief. The port bulwarks from the main to the fore-rigging had been carried away even to the deck. Spare spars had to be fastened there by ropes until we got into port. The second mate said it was my fault on account of bad steering.

One day all hands were busy bailing water and guano out of the hold. I was at the wheel again, trying my best to steer straight. It was of no use; the old tub yawed around and was struck by a heavy sea. A large quantity of water went down the scuttle and made more mud, all of which had to be bailed out. How everybody did swear and growl! But I derived some consolation on account of the second mate being nearly killed. The water had knocked him off his feet and dashed him against the bulwarks. When he came aft, rubbing his arms and legs, I had to grin. That was the only time I ever felt really happy on that packet. Shortly afterwards he took the wheel and sent me to help the bucket brigade. Very soon the brig yawed again. I knew what would happen when I saw a heavy wave coming, so got down the scuttle and shut it very quickly. After the commotion was all over I got on deck. Very much to my joy, the starboard bulwarks had been carried away. My friend the second mate had nothing to say about bad steering after that.

CHAPTER VI
THE FLYING DUTCHMAN

THAT night we were compelled to heave to, for the waves were almost sinking us. At two o'clock in the morning my chum was to relieve me at the wheel. He was rather slow about doing it, too, as it was very comfortable for him in the galley. I was about played out holding the helm hard down, there being no steerage-way, as we were drifting to the leeward. Our object was to keep the vessel head on to the seas as nearly as possible, so as to ride over them as they came along. So much guano had been taken from the forehold that it caused the brig to settle by the stern and raise the forward part up, consequently every time the bow dipped into a wave the water which came over would rush aft on the deck, strike the taffrail, and give the man at the wheel a good shower-bath. That happened every few minutes. Between drenchings we had the cold wind for a variety. The ship's clock was in the cabin skylight, visible to the helmsman, whose duty it was to strike the bell one stroke for every half hour. At four bells he was to be relieved; at eight bells the watches would change; thus it would be four hours on deck and four hours below until we arrived in port. Now I had been watching the clock very anxiously for two hours, my whole body stiff and numb with the cold and wet. Nearly a half hour after the right time, my friend Jimmy very reluctantly made his appearance. I waited until he had hold of the wheel and then I chided him in very impolite language. When I had said everything that I could think of to hurt his feelings I stopped. In the meantime I was holding on to a rope and sharing the shower-baths with him. It helped to loosen my jaws, at any rate, even if it did no other good.

The cook's galley is a small house built on deck, in size about four by six feet, with a sliding door on each side, the one to windward being always kept shut except in very fine weather. Now I was hustling along as fast as my stiff joints would allow me to get into the galley. There, at least, I would be sheltered from the cold winds. I had got inside and was turning to close the door, when I saw a sight which simply paralyzed me. A large full-rigged ship with squared yards, all sails set, even to the royals and studding-sails rigged out on both sides, was coming straight for us, and distant only a few hundred yards. Our brig, being hove to, was helpless to get out of the way. Certain destruction seemed inevitable, with no possible hope of escaping a speedy death. I yelled out at the top of my voice, "A ship on the lee beam!" Jimmy, at the wheel, got a glimpse of the ship, and let out a yelp that brought the mate on deck. The mate, who had been loafing in the cabin and shirking his duty, also did some tall yelping when he saw our danger.

There was no chance to get on our knees to pray then. The decks were too wet and slippery, besides, we had to use our hands to keep from being washed overboard. As we could not do the proper thing in orthodox style, we did some tall cursing, as being the next best thing under the circumstances. Swearing is a sailor's balm for many ills.

We were terribly excited; only a few seconds and all would be over with us. Our brig was drifting north at the rate of three miles an hour. The strange vessel was heading south in that gale and with all sails set; she should have been racing through the water at a twenty-knots rate. You can imagine our surprise when we observed that the other vessel was rapidly going backward and disappearing in a hazy mist. Suddenly there was a break in the clouds, and we had a glimpse of the full moon for a few minutes, for the first time in several weeks, although the nights were nearly twenty hours in length. Soon we were in darkness again. That was our first experience with the ship Flying Dutchman. The whole affair had happened so suddenly and unexpectedly that we had no time to think. The idea of a ship carrying all sail in that gale was ridiculous, but to sail dead against the wind was still more so. We were very much disgusted with ourselves for being so badly fooled, but, at the same time, we were a greatly scared lot of sailors. The explanation was simple enough. The clouds were black and heavy, flying low down near the water. A rift in them allowed the moon to shine dimly between the edges and cause the illusion. A few nights afterward we were running before the wind. All hands were close-reefing the main top-sail. Off the port bow we saw what appeared to be a ship on fire. Our course was altered to that direction, and it proved to be the old Dutchman again. At last the gale from the south broke up. We had got into the "pamperos"—westerly winds from Buenos Ayres. The days were increasing in length, and the weather became much warmer. The wind being on our beam, we could steer straight, compared with what we had been doing before the wind. Besides, the heavy rolling and lurching had diminished greatly. The effect of heavy cargo, so much below the water-line, was greatly counteracted by the wind striking us sideways. Going before the wind, the old brig rolled terribly at times—so much so that we often expected the masts to be snapped off, on account of the sudden jerking from side to side. The forecastle was always wet and muddy, and, while eating, we would sit on a chest, holding our pans in our laps, a cup in one hand, and conveying the food to our mouths with the other, with both heels firmly braced on the deck. Time and again an extra lurch would send us a-sliding to the other side, bang against a chest or bunk, the food flying in every direction. Back and forth we would go a dozen times before we could stop. The sulphur and brimstone would hang in festoons from the deck beams by the time we had stopped cursing the old brig.

On the first clear day, instead of going to bed in my morning watch below, eight to twelve in the morning, I went aloft to the fore-top, and remained there the four hours enjoying the luxury of an airy wind-bath. It was the first time in nearly three months that my clothing was dry, and not so very dry then, either. The mates had been throwing out hints about going into port for repairs. We had passed all the Pacific harbours, and were doing the same with the Atlantic harbours, when, very much to our joy, we sighted the Sugar Loaf, a very high conical rock, it being the southern point of land at the entrance to the harbour of Rio de Janeiro—River of January—Brazil, South America. So, much to our joy, we were bound for port. My chum and I were of one mind—that was, to quit the guano business P. D. Q.

The entrance to the harbour was very narrow and well fortified. There were steep rocks on each side. We were hailed from one of the forts and asked the brig's name, destination, and last port. Our sails were gradually taken in. At last we rounded to and dropped anchor. Rio is admitted by all sailors to be the finest harbour in the world, and I will guarantee that our old tub of a brig was the most dilapidated and dirtiest specimen of the shipbuilder's handicraft that ever anchored in it. It is a generally well-founded belief among sailors that rats will desert a sinking ship. We often remarked that a rat had not been seen on the Grenfalls during the voyage. I must say the rodents made a very close calculation, if that was the reason for at some time quitting their cosy quarters. My first act in port was to tie a rope around my wet blankets and lower them into the water. By swashing them up and down for awhile, I got considerable of the mud removed. Hanging in the hot sun, they became dry by evening. So I enjoyed a good night's sleep on deck. It was quite a contrast from what I had been doing for weeks past—namely, getting into a soaking wet bed with all my clothes on, dripping with water, and the sea dropping on me in small instalments through the leaky decks.

Our worthy captain was an entirely different man from what he was at sea in the Cape Horn regions. Warm weather, with no danger to be feared, made quite an improvement in his personal appearance. He was also more self-important and domineering. The two mates and he were small men, about five feet two inches in height. The way in which they murdered the Queen's English was something simply terrible. "Mike, 'ow's 'er 'ead?" was the question often asked at the wheel when they wished to know the point of the compass I was steering, so as to enter it in the log-book. The disabled condition of the brig had been reported to the English consul. He appointed three ship captains to "survey" our vessel, and report whether it was seaworthy or not. They came on board and examined everything. We, the sailors, took our knives and showed them how rotten the remaining bulwarks were, how the decks leaked; in fact, we did all we could to get the old tub condemned. It was estimated that one hundred tons of guano had been dumped overboard; however, nothing was said about the quantity of water that went with it. The captains looked very wise, but said nothing. Finally, they got into their boats and returned to shore. My shipmates and myself were in great hope that the vessel would be condemned as unseaworthy. That meant our release and three months' extra pay on account of being discharged in a foreign port. Greatly to our disgust, the report was briefly: "The brig Grenfalls, with necessary repairs, is fit to continue the voyage."

In a few days we hoisted anchor and sailed up to a small island close to the city. After considerable trouble we got the old tub fastened to a small dock. Then we were allowed time to dispose of a mighty poor dinner. All the remaining guano was to be taken out and placed on the dock, a job which we did not like. Jim and myself, while eating, had a quiet talk on the chances of getting our discharge from the vessel. We both decided to declare war. No more guano work for us! We were eating our last dinner on that boat, but we did not know it then. The war took place in earnest, and most unexpectedly. Two explanations are necessary before I proceed with the narrative. There was an able seaman in the other watch, more intelligent than the average English sailor. His vessel had been wrecked on the Pacific coast, and he had shipped with us in order to return to England and sail in his former employer's service again. From him I learned some facts in regard to English marine law. English sailors always carry large jack-knives, a shackle at the butt end, to which is fastened a lanyard, the latter going around the neck. The knife, when not in use, is stuck in the waistband of the trousers. With American sailors, a long knife, carried in a sheath and strapped around the waist, is the fashion. It is a very necessary and useful article on shipboard, used in cutting food—there are no forks—scraping masts, repairing rigging, and so forth. It is always ready for instant use in case of danger or accident. After dinner we had plenty of work to do. Towards evening extra lines from the bow and stern were run ashore and fastened to large rocks. Old canvas was cut in narrow strips and wound around the ropes in every place where they were liable to chafe on the sharp stones on the beach. We were still at that work at nine o'clock, with no sign of supper yet. I made up my mind to quit work, and had just got on deck when I heard the first mate and Jimmy talking rather loudly by the cabin door. Too much work and nothing to eat was the cause of the row. My chum was mad all over. Suddenly the mate caught him by each wrist and gave his arms a quick, downward jerk. It was an old trick, and very painful to a person whose arms were hanging down loosely. In an instant Jimmy had his knife open and made a lunge for the mate. The lanyard prevented the free action of the knife, but the blade had scratched the skin on the mate's throat and made a long cut in the neck of his tight-fitting, heavy knit undershirt. The mate began to run and yell "Murder!" Around the deck he sprinted, with my chum after him. Every few steps Jimmy would make a dig at him with the knife, only to receive himself a jerk in the back of the neck from the lanyard. There was an old box on the main hatch. Without being noticed by any of us, our old enemy—the red-headed cook—was standing on it, with an iron bolt in his hand. The mate took in the situation, though, and, on the last lap, he crossed the deck at the main hatch. As Jimmy came along, the cook hit him a whack on the head with the piece of iron that laid my poor friend on the deck *hors de combat*. The cook had no time to gloat over his victory. He was howling out, "Wurrah, wurrah!" and made remarkably quick time for the cabin, landing below without his feet touching the stairs. A sailor was after him with a sheath-knife minus the lanyard attachment. Our disabled shipmate was carried forward and laid on deck. Having no fine Turkish sponges or decorated wash-bowls, we could not dress his head according to modern style. We did the best we could, however, which was to lower a bucket over the vessel's side and fill it with dirty sea water. His head received several good bathings. The treatment was liberal and heroic, the contents of a full bucket being dumped on him at a time. It helped to revive him and to wash off the blood, simultaneously.

At last success rewarded our efforts. The patient sat up. When he had got the salt water out of his mouth, he wanted to know "what in —— we were trying to do with him?" It being nearly ten o'clock, all hands concluded to have supper. The cook was afraid to come on deck, so we went to the galley and took all the food in sight. It was carried into the forecastle. The chandelier—a tin cup full of grease with a rag for a wick—was trimmed and lighted. Our frugal repast was interrupted by the captain's sticking his head down the scuttle and inquiring if Jimmy wanted a bandage and salve for his head. Jimmy very curtly told him to "Go to ——." The captain was desirous that the crew should desert and forfeit the money due to them, for he could get other men for one third of the amount we were getting. Nine dollars a month for ordinary, and eleven dollars a month for able seamen was the rate in Rio; while our pay from Callao was twenty-five dollars and thirty-five dollars per month. My chum and I had about forty dollars due to each of us, and I intended to get it if possible. The rest of the men wanted to remain on the vessel on account of the big wages, and the hardest part of the voyage being over. Immediately after breakfast the next morning Jimmy and I went aft and called for the captain. We requested permission to see the English consul, but received an evasive answer. It was to be a game of bluff beyond all doubt, so my recently acquired knowledge of marine law was to be tested. I stated plainly to the captain that seamen were allowed by law to see the consul "if they had any complaints to make." We demanded to be at once taken to the consul's office, as we were not satisfied with our food and treatment, and wished for an investigation. We said that he would have trouble if he refused to comply with the law. Very reluctantly, he told us to get into the ship's boat, and we rowed over to the city. On landing, he gave directions to the consul's office, where, on arriving, we found that the captain had taken a short cut and got there ahead of us. Consequently the consul gave us a very cool reception and asked us what we wanted of him. He got a brief synopsis of the trip around the Cape to commence with, then a description of the food, next of the short allowance of water; and last, we charged the captain with ignoring the law in regard to giving each man the legal allowance of lime-juice a day.[C]

[C] Years ago canned vegetables and fruit were unknown at sea; for that reason lime-juice was served to the men daily, as a preventive of scurvy. English vessels were nicknamed "lime-juicers" on that account.

The captain had considerable to say, himself. At last the consul refused to discharge us. We were informed that we should have better food for the future. The captain smiled with satisfaction, for a short time only. All was not over yet. My last card was to be played and it won. "Well, Consul, this man and I do not propose to go back to the captain's old tub. We volunteer for Her Majesty's service!"

The consul laughed, and informed the captain that he would be expected at the office at two o'clock in the afternoon with our discharges and the money which was due us.

What clothing we had was badly rotted by the effect of salt water and guano; therefore we had no reason to return to the Grenfalls for our old rags. Out of the office we went in high glee. The first sailor I met on the street gave us directions to a sailors' boarding-house. Portuguese Joe was the landlord's title. No time was lost in making his acquaintance. The mere fact that we were two sailors to be paid off that day was sufficient recommendation.

CHAPTER VII
IN HER MAJESTY'S SERVICE

NO money in advance, nor baggage as security for our board, was required. Nothing in the house was too good for us; we could have anything we wanted, and, oh, how glad the other boarders were to see us! I almost felt at that time as if I had met about twenty long-lost brothers. All that affection cost Jimmy and me several rounds of drink for the "house." That afternoon we went to the consulate and received our discharges and pay. The money was in Brazilian currency, and, together, our money amounted to a hundred and fifty-five thousand reis—twenty reis equal to a cent of United States money. Bookkeeping in that country requires the use of a large number of figures.

Our first venture was to get new suits of clothes and enjoy the luxury of a much-needed fresh-water bath, when "Richard was himself again." What a change in our mode of living! Fruit of all kinds to be had for almost nothing; comfortable beds to sleep in; fresh food and vegetables to eat. The only thing I objected to was that we had too many newly found friends. I was strictly temperate at that time. Jimmy made me his banker, with the condition that I should give him money only in small amounts.

Brazil is a very large country, and at that time was the only empire in South America. Dom Pedro III was emperor. His palace was close to the city of Rio. I saw him several times, as he frequently rode through the city in his carriage, always escorted by his bodyguard of thirty cavalrymen. He was a very fine-looking young man with fair complexion. No doubt he was the most progressive ruler Brazil ever had. Now he is dead and Brazil is a Republic. Rio de Janeiro is the capital, and a most beautiful city it is. Viewing it from the bay in the night-time, it resembles the dress-circle in an immensely large theatre, the street-lights forming the rows of seats. The language is Portuguese, much similar to Spanish. I had very little difficulty in making myself understood when conversing with the natives. There was not a sewer in the city. Large tubs about three feet high, eighteen inches in diameter, were used in the houses for all refuse and waste material, and, when filled, they were carried on the heads of slaves at night-time and emptied into the bay. A large building at the water's edge was the public dumping ground. The slaves were nearly all genuine Africans, naked to the waist, the breast and face tattooed in different designs, by scarring the skin with a knife.

When one of those fellows came down the street on a dog-trot, singing "Hoo! hoo! hoo! hoo!" I would get out of his way quickly. It was a wonder to me how they could balance those heavy tubs on their heads and keep swinging their arms at the same time.

The native liquor is cashass, distilled from sugar-cane. Take equal parts of pure alcohol and water, put in a very liberal quantity of creosote, and you will have a good sample of cashass—flavour, smell, and strength will be the same as the genuine article. One evening, on returning to the boarding-house, there was quite an excitement in the dining-room. My friend Jimmy was laid out on the table, with three men holding him down; he was in spasms and frothing at the mouth. My impression was that he had been poisoned. After a while he quieted down and went to sleep. The next morning he confidentially remarked to me that he had no more use for any of "that —— cashass." My reason for describing the liquor is to give an idea of its strength. Once, when I was on an English man-of-war, it was probably the cause of a friend's being drowned and of getting me into a serious scrape.

I would frequently take a stroll down to the military dock where the boat from the man-of-war landed. It was interesting to observe the peculiarities of the different nationalities. The Americans were the most intelligent, very neat in appearance, their clothing of fine material and well made, dark blue flannel shirts embroidered with black silk, a white silk star on each corner of the wide collars, a silk ribbon with the name of the ship in gilt letters on the sailor hats. When their boats landed the officers would get out, then the boat's crew, with the exception of one man, going where they pleased, returning after a time, and pulling off to their ship. Next were the Englishmen. Their clothes fitted awkwardly. In appearance they were not so bright and cheerful. No going ashore for them! A midshipman was always in charge of the boat, every man being required to remain in his seat. The Italians, Spanish, French, and Brazilians were a dirty, barefooted lot, probably not one in ten being able to read or write. The English always had difficulty in getting men for the navy. Low wages, flogging with the cat-o'-nine-tails, and no chance for promotion, were the chief reasons. A law was passed allowing any seaman in the British merchant service to volunteer in any part of the world for Her Majesty's service. That was the reason why I got my discharge from the Grenfalls. I remained at Portuguese Joe's for two weeks, my money being spent in sight-seeing. Then I went on board Her Majesty's frigate Madagascar and shipped for five years as an ordinary seaman. My pay was one pound sixteen shillings—about nine dollars—a month.

I had to retain the name of Mike Murray on account of the discharge from the last ship. Cloth was furnished to me—flannel and other articles—for clothing, everything being charged to me excepting hammock and bag. With the assistance of the other sailors, I soon had clothing made and became a full-fledged man-of-war's-man. The Madagascar was a very large frigate with two tiers of guns, and had been stationed at Rio for a number of years without leaving the harbour. The admiral of the South Atlantic station made her the flagship of the fleet. Only about one third of the full complement of men was on board, and, consequently, we had no drilling at the big guns or making and furling sails. But we had "holystoning" decks enough to make up for it. At four o'clock every morning we were routed out of hammocks to wash decks. Sand and a little water would be sprinkled on the deck, each man would have a piece of flat sandstone, and then, on our knees, we would do some mighty hard scouring, hence the name of "holystoning." Afterwards, with the use of plenty of water, the sand and dirt would be washed off. Then, with swabs, the deck would be dried and afterwards swept with brooms. By that time it would be seven o'clock, and then we had breakfast.

Jimmy came on board and shipped a few days after myself. We both belonged to the same mess. He had a picnic, as I gave him my share of grog to drink. Each mess was composed of fourteen men, each man in turn being cook of the mess for one day. His work was to set the table, draw rations, and bring the food from the galley. At twelve-thirty he would take a bucket and get the grog. The grog was one half gill of Jamaica rum and three half gills of water, mixed, making one half pint. Each mess had a measure holding a little less than that quantity. The cook would give each man his allowance, and the difference in the measures after fourteen men had been served would be considerable; that would be the cook's perquisite. Orders had been given to refit the Madagascar with entirely new rigging. The Brazilian Government had given permission to use one of their ship-houses to work in. Every day a gang of us were taken ashore to fit up the standing rigging. We were at that work for two months. The experience and knowledge I acquired in that brief time made me a good sailor. The English Government had the lease of a small island in the harbour on which were erected a number of buildings containing supplies for the navy. As we returned to the ship at night, our boat would stop there and bring off the paymaster. One evening we had to wait for him. As was the English custom, the boat was rowed a few hundred yards from the dock, then "Peak oars!" was the order, each man holding his oar straight up, the handle resting on the bottom of the boat, the blade in the air. It was the second cutter with fourteen oars, two men on each seat, quite a fine sight, but very tedious for the men. We had a sudden change from the sublime to the ridiculous that time. Two of the crew had got into an argument. One of them, getting excited, emphasized his remarks by lifting his oar and bringing it down on the bottom of the boat. That ended the debate abruptly. The boat, being old and rotten, could not stand such treatment. The force of the blow knocked a big hole in the bottom. In a few seconds all hands were in the water, men and oars badly mixed up. Those of us who could swim struck out for dry land, the remainder saving themselves by clinging to the wreck.

We had very little work to do after the old frigate was newly rigged. I would look out of the gun-ports and watch the shipping in the harbour. One day the United States brig Perry came in from a cruise on the African coast and anchored close to us. She was a beautiful vessel. All the crew appeared to be happy and contented. They were a fine, active lot of men. I should have liked to exchange places with any of them. Finally they went on another cruise in quest of slavers. The next time I saw the Perry was in Boston during the war, and I was then one of her officers, in a position I little dreamed of holding when I watched her leaving the harbour of Rio de Janeiro.

I soon became discontented and homesick on the old frigate. My messmates, knowing me to be a "blawsted Yankee," as they called me, made me ill-natured. I usually returned what they gave. After several fights they let me alone, but I was punished by being put on the black-list for fighting. That meant being kept at work all day long cleaning brass-work, etc. At dinner hour I would be on the quarter-deck with my bowl of grog, an extra half pint of water being introduced, and I then received a spoon with holes in it with which to sup the grog. With my cap under my arm, I would be ordered to drink Her Majesty's health. It was a tedious job sipping that infernal stuff out of the bowl with the spoon. It would run out as fast as I dipped it up. Sometimes there would be ten or twelve men undergoing the same punishment. In the evening I would have to stand one hour on the quarter-deck, toeing one of the seams. Poor Jimmy got into a scrape, so I had him drinking Her Majesty's health with me. This was also the case with a half-breed American Indian from Massachusetts, and a greenhorn from England, and a very troublesome quartette we proved to be. That night all four of us deserted. The first lieutenant had his gig condemned and got a new one to replace it. While we were doing the seam-toeing act he came on deck and ordered us to get into the new gig and pull around the ship, so that he could see how it set in the water. A conversation between us while rowing made it plain that all were anxious to run away. We went on the gun deck and had a quiet talk. Everything was arranged for going ashore. The boat could not be hoisted up, as there were no spare davits for it. That just suited us.

At bedtime we got into our hammocks with our clothes on, and about three o'clock we got our bags containing all our clothing and took them on the gun deck. Matt, the half-breed, got into the boat from the gun ports and hauled it around to the bow port. The bags were then handed down. Jimmy had gone back for something and we were waiting for him. At last he came and handed me a pocket-book. All of us got into the boat, and away we went. No one had seen us leaving. There were three decks in that frigate, the spar, the gun, and the lower or berth deck. The crew swung their hammocks on the latter. What few officers and men there were on duty at night would be on the spar deck, so there was no one on the gun deck to bother us, and all below were asleep. Had there been a full crew, arrangements would have been different and our plan frustrated. When we got into the city, Matt and the greenhorn went ashore. Jimmy and I concluded to take a trip up the bay. By seven o'clock we were quite a distance from the city. The boat was run ashore and our bags were taken out. The dry land was good enough for us. Something to eat was next in order. The pocket-book was then examined and found to contain eighty thousand reis, Brazilian money—forty dollars. Then Jimmy explained how he got it. A new man slept next to my worthy chum, and every night he would place his pocket-book between the mattress and the canvas hammock, and lie on the whole affair himself, feeling secure against all loss. Just where the pocket-book lay there was a lump bulging out in the canvas, so Jim cut a slit in the right place and the booty was his.

A short distance from the landing-place were a number of slaughter-houses, and the butchers were very much surprised to see two man-of-war's-men with their baggage in their neighbourhood. One of their number could speak Spanish, so a friendly conversation took place which ended in their purchasing our clothes—bags and all. We received a fair price, both parties being satisfied with the bargain. After eating a good breakfast in one of their houses, we bade our new acquaintances good-bye. With plenty of money in our pockets, and on shore, everything seemed quite pleasant. Our plans were soon agreed upon—to take a walking tour to the south, have a view of the country, get to the seaport of St. Catharines, and ship on some vessel for the United States. It was necessary to make a détour of the city to get on our right road. After awhile we met a market-woman with fruit and bought enough for our dinner. Sitting under a tree, we enjoyed our picnic very much. All our money was then counted; there proved to be one hundred and seventy thousand reis altogether. A fourteen-thousand-reis bill I put inside the lining of my hat, the balance in my pocket. During the rest, Jim proposed going into the city to make some purchases for our journey. We went—and that was a grand mistake. When we passed the Hamburg House, kept by a Dutchman, we were reminded that we were thirsty, so we went in and sat down at a table and ordered a bottle of English ale. Just then I noticed a young fellow go out of the door. After awhile I asked about the ale—why they did not bring it? They replied that they had to send out for it. Shortly afterwards the English consul's "runner" came in with two vigilantes and, pointing to us, said, "Esas dos"—"Those two." That settled it! We had been "given away" for the reward, three pounds sterling—about fifteen dollars each—being the amount for apprehension of deserters from Her Majesty's service, and off to the calaboose we were marched. About twelve hours' liberty on shore was all we had enjoyed. We were taken into the office and searched, and the money was taken out of my pocket and carefully counted. They gave me a receipt for it. Very greatly to their disgust, no big bank roll was found on my chum. I never saw a cent of that money again. Our loss was somebody's gain that time, sure enough. We were put into a cell with about fifteen other prisoners, among them two sailors, deserters, from the English sloop-of-war Siren. From them we found out the rules of our new quarters. No food was furnished to prisoners—either to buy it, or have friends bring it, was the custom. As they had been locked up for two days without food, they had a yearning for something to eat. I called the turnkey and made him understand in Spanish that I wanted coffee and rolls for four. In Portuguese he made me understand that money would have to be furnished first. I showed the receipt for money in the office, but that would not do, so I took the fourteen-thousand-reis bill out of my cap and handed it to him. He gave a queer, astonished look and then a sickly smile, but we got the coffee and rolls, however. That little luncheon cost me just two thousand reis. I considered myself lucky to get the change back. They got nearly all of it, though, the next day. Finally, we four deserters were taken outside the city limits and, much to our surprise, landed in the penitentiary. Not having committed any crime against the country, or having had a trial, we found ourselves convicts "doing time" for nothing.

CHAPTER VIII
THE CAT-O'-NINE-TAILS

NO red tape was wasted upon us. The formalities were few. Being taken into a small building, we took off all our clothing, which was tied in bundles with our names on them; then, after we had each received a pair of blue overalls and a blue shirt, the change was complete. Barefooted and bareheaded, we were marched to the cell houses and locked up. Food was scarce the first day. We had nothing to eat, as no rations had been issued for us. The second day only one meal was provided, a small one at that. The third day, however, we would get all the law allowed. My appetite was getting quite keen about this time. When the prospect of getting something to eat looked promising, they found out that a slight mistake had been made in our case.

The English consul had leased a small building on the premises as a lock-up for British sailors who got into trouble or refused to do duty on their respective ships. When the vessels were ready for sea, the sailors would be put on board and all the expenses deducted from their wages. So we were dressed up again and marched over to the consul's pen. The same trouble about the food occurred there. If they had made just one more mistake we certainly should have starved to death. In a few days we were marched to the consulate and then returned to the Madagascar. Our experience on shore had been a novelty but not entirely a pleasant one. A warm reception was given us on the frigate—twenty-eight days each of solitary confinement on bread and water, twenty-one days on the black-list and lying in irons from sunset until sunrise. The value of the lost boat and all expenses, including the reward, was to be deducted from our wages, and, besides, we would have to pay for a new outfit of clothing. At nine dollars a month, it would be some time before our accounts would be squared up. Jim and I swore point-blank that we knew nothing about the boat, and they never got it back. Somebody was ahead a new boat, anyhow. I never paid my share of the loss, either. Matt, the half-breed, was caught in a coffee-saloon before ten o'clock of the same morning and at once taken back to the ship. On our arrival he was doing "solitary." The greenhorn was the only one of the party to get away. Aft, on the lower or third deck, was the midshipmen's and clerks' mess-room, on one side of the deck. Abaft that was a bulkhead or partition which left a space to the stern that was used as a store-room for the admiral's and captain's supplies. In there was also a room used as the "solitary." Forward of the partition was where the prisoners were kept in irons. Iron bars ten feet in length, a knot on one end, a padlock on the other, and a big lot of shackles completed the outfit. The men would sit on deck in a row, each one placing a shackle on each ankle. The first man would run the end of the bar through the eyes of his shackle and then the next would do the same, the padlock was fastened, and we would be secure for the night. The bar lay underneath, resting on deck. Walking or standing was impossible. The midshipmen and clerks swung their hammocks above us. Once in a while we would rap on the partition and, through the crack, would inquire about Matt's health and comfort, "If the hardtack and water agreed with him, and how would he like a nice beefsteak?" As Matt was in the "solitary," Jim and I had to wait for our turn. So we were doing the black-list and iron punishment together. About the time my black-list was half over I got into more trouble.

The captain lived on shore, near the Sugar Loaf. His boat had left the ship and some article which he wanted had been forgotten. Such a dereliction was simply terrible. The captain of a man-of-war in those days was a trifle more despotic than the Czar of Russia. A cutter with fourteen oars was "called away" in a hurry to rectify the mistake, but a man was short for the crew. The lieutenant gave orders for some one to get into the boat. Just then I was working by the companion-way—the ladder on ship's side. Much to my surprise, I was told to be more active in obeying orders and to get into the cutter. I did so. My being a prisoner at the time seemed not to have been taken into consideration. It was quite a distance to shore down the bay. The man next me on the thwart gave me a nudge and said, "Mike, my mon, show 'em your 'eels on shore." The others near me also had something to say, much to my annoyance, as I did not want any one to suspect what my intentions were. We landed soon after the captain's boat did. There being no midshipman in the cutter, we all stepped on shore. One of the men spoke to the coxswain in a low tone, and I was ordered back into the cutter. I refused and stated that I was going to a saloon for a drink. I walked away rather quickly. Looking back, I saw that all the men excepting one were running after me. Then I ran as fast as possible towards a steep rocky hill. I was gaining on them rapidly. Some perpendicular rocks prevented my going farther in that direction. Then I turned around, intending to run down the hill and break through the crowd for another race. Just as I got near them, I stumbled, falling on my face and rolling over into a hole full of muddy water. I was badly hurt and my nose was bleeding freely. They took me to the cutter and pulled off to the frigate.

On our arrival all had to go on deck and stand in a line toeing a seam, to be searched for smuggled liquor by the ship's corporal, the lieutenant looking on. Then the coxswain reported me for attempting to run away. The lieutenant saw that I was covered with mud and blood. He asked me if the report was true. I answered "Yes," and told him that the whole boat's crew were a dirty lot of curs for bringing me back after inducing me to run. The lieutenant looked at them all slowly, and then at me. With a contemptuous sneer, he said, "Thank you, men," and sent them forward, at the same time ordering me to be put in irons. The ship's corporal led me away below, at the same time growling about the trouble he was having on my account. About half an hour afterward my old friend, the corporal, made his appearance. He released me from irons and escorted me on deck. The lieutenant asked me if I was badly hurt, and all particulars in regard to my running away. Much to my surprise, he told me to resume my work, that he was to blame in a measure himself, as he had no right to allow a prisoner to leave the ship.

My first business was to see the coxswain and some of the boat's crew and give them a good plain cursing. In a few days afterward, Matt's time in the "solitary" expired and I was locked up in his place. One half pound of hardtack per day and one quart of water was my allowance. Nothing very interesting occurred during the time, excepting once when the captain's steward came into the store-room one day for some wine. He spoke to me through the small iron-barred window which was in the partition on the store-room side. He told me to get my tin cup and hold it up to the bars. With a piece of paper he made a funnel and filled my cup full of good sherry wine. Crackers and raisins were also given me, so I had a high old time all to myself that day. The twenty-eight days expired and all my punishment was over. Jimmy relieved me, and when he went into the door it was the last time we ever saw each other. After all the hard times and many scrapes we had got into together, we parted without a chance to shake hands. I never heard of him afterward. Twice while in Liverpool, England, I went to his address, 17 Lower Frederick Street, but no one knew anything about him.

Matt, the half-breed, and I got to be friendly and both of us were determined to get away from the frigate. Our only chance was to swim ashore, we not being trusted in any of the boats. It was necessary to wait for a night when there would be no moon and a flood-tide running in from the sea. In the meantime, to avert suspicion, I started making my new clothing. The blue cloth for my best trousers at Government prices was one pound sterling. That I had smuggled from the ship and on shore, to be sold. I was to receive half of what it would sell for. In a few days I received five milreis and a long skin of cashass. The cashass is put in skins such as are used for bologna sausage. In that form it can easily be secreted about a sailor's clothing and smuggled on board. The cashass I gave to Matt for safe-keeping, as we should need a good drink before taking our long swim. The five milreis in silver I put in a small bag hanging round my neck. Every night we would sneak up to the gun deck. The prospects not being favourable, we would postpone our trip. One night while I was awake, the ship's corporal came to my hammock with a lantern in his hands. He took a look at me and then went away. I knew then that our plan to go was known. After that I remained in my hammock and let Matt do the prospecting. Finally, one morning, we concluded to make the attempt that night. During the day I had my bag from the rack to do some sewing, and Matt came to me with a blue flannel shirt and asked me to put it in my bag for a while, which, unfortunately, I did. That night the corporal came to my hammock twice before midnight; then I dozed off to sleep and was awakened by some one feeling my face. It was Matt. He was quite drunk and insisted upon my taking a drink from the skin. He said he was then going to the gun deck to get a rope ready for getting into the water and would return for me when all was ready. That was the last I saw of him. I waited for a while. The effects of the strong liquor put me into a sound sleep. The next thing I knew was that the crew were holystoning the gun deck. The noise of the stones right over my head had awakened me. I put on my clothes and tried to sneak in among them unobserved, but the attempt was a failure. The boatswain saw me. "Hello, Mike, where did you come from? I thought you had gone ashore with Matt," was the salute I received.

It seems that when all hands were called, we were missed at once. Matt's hammock, being the nearest, was examined. He being gone, it was concluded that I was with him. I tried to play innocent, but it was of no use. After breakfast I was ordered before the first lieutenant and reported for not turning out to scrub decks, and then for aiding and abetting desertion. My bag was brought from the rack and examined. The blue cloth was missing. A stolen shirt, with the owner's name under the collar, was found. Matt stole that shirt. It was the one he had asked me to keep for him. Conduct detrimental to discipline in Her Majesty's service was another charge. The lieutenant then laid down the law to me in splendid style, and ended thus: "Now, Michael Murray, you have made considerable trouble on this frigate, and I shall see that you get 'four dozen.' Then you can desert— that is, if you get the chance. Corporal, put him in irons." When the corporal put the padlock on the bar, he said: "Mike, my lad, you're in for it now!"

About five days afterward I was taken on the quarter-deck again. The lieutenant wanted to know who brought the cashass on board to Matt and myself. I replied that I knew nothing about it and that I had never seen Matt with the liquor in his possession. Then I was told that Matt's body had been found floating in the bay. He had on all his clothes excepting cap and shoes. Inside of his shirt was found the skin containing a small quantity of cashass. He must have been quite drunk or he would not have tried to swim such a distance with his clothes on; or it may be that he fell overboard and that that was the reason he did not come back for me as he promised.

"Four dozen" on an English man-of-war means flogging with the cat-o'-nine-tails. The "cat" is a hardwood handle eighteen inches long, to one end of which are attached nine pieces of hard lines, about one eighth of an inch in diameter and eighteen inches long. At the end of each tail is a hard knot. When punishment is to be inflicted the "tails" are soaked in strong brine. That makes them hard and heavy. A wooden grating from a hatchway is placed on end, resting against the bulwarks. All hands are called to witness punishment. Everybody must be present, from the captain to the powder boys. The prisoner is stripped naked to the waist, his feet are lashed to the bottom of the grating, and his arms are stretched out full length and fastened. The face and breast are then close to the grating, with no chance remaining of moving the body. The ship's surgeon watches to see that the prisoner does not die while being punished. The boatswain's mate is on the left side. He swings the "cat" over his head with the right hand, at the same time drawing the tails through his left hand. At every stroke nine stripes are cut on the prisoner's back, the knots at the same time making little holes in the skin, about two seconds elapsing between each stroke. After two dozen strokes have been given, the boatswain's mate steps to the other side of the prisoner and gives the remaining two dozen, the skin being cut by that means into diamond-shaped pieces. By the time the punishment is over the man will be covered with blood and greatly exhausted.

I had been keeping very quiet for the last few days in order to avert suspicion. I had been examining the old shackles, and found two that would release me from the bar at any time. One was quite large. By taking off my shoe I could squeeze my foot from the bar. The other shackle must have been an odd one, as it had extra large eyes, and would slip nicely over the knob at the end of the bar. I laid them on the deck to have them handy, then I sent for the corporal to take me to the water-closet. When I returned I picked up the shackles that I wanted and placed them over my ankles. When he had gone I put all the other shackles away out of reach so there could be no mixing up. My mind rested easy then. I was having a chance to go before the flogging, instead of after, as the lieutenant proposed. At last, the day for my punishment was set. The captain had come on board the frigate and my conduct was reported. I was brought before him and the charges read to me. Orders were given to have me flogged with the "Thieves'" cat-o'-nine-tails at eight o'clock the next morning. "Four dozen lashes on the bare back." The "Thieves' cat" meant two knots in the tail instead of one. I was to receive extra punishment for a crime I never committed, but the finding of the shirt in my bag had been sufficient.

CHAPTER IX
THE ESCAPE

WHEN the corporal took me below again I asked him to let me get some clean clothes from my bag. I selected a pair of white duck trousers and a white shirt. I wanted the lightest suit that I could get. The corporal probably thought that I intended dressing neatly for the whipping in the morning. I was very particular in putting the shackles on my ankles, the one with the large eyes going on the left leg, so as to be at the knob end of the bar. The big one went on the right leg. I could not prevent myself from grinning while he was so carefully locking the end of the bar. He gave the lock an extra pull, to satisfy himself that it was fast, and walked off. My hammock, instead of being lashed up sideways, as customary, was merely rolled loosely and left on deck, so that I could spread it out for sleeping at night-time. I made a sort of lounge with it and took life easy, for the time being. At nine in the evening, the midshipmen and clerks got into their hammocks, leaving their clothes on top of their sea-chests. I spread out my bed and lay down. My position had to be straight out, on my back, as the iron bar had to be taken into consideration. Soon all but myself were asleep. Time passed very slowly. I knew the corporal would have a look at me about midnight and that then I should be ready for my trip. I could tell the time by hearing the ship's bell striking every half hour. About one in the morning, I was getting very uneasy in my mind, as I knew it was about time for the tide to change and run out to sea—a very serious matter for me. At last my friend made his appearance. Everything was secure and satisfactory, so he went away. Then I commenced operations. First, I got out of the shackles, and taking off all my clothing, tied it in a neat, flat bundle. My money and knife I left hanging to my neck. Next I gathered up some clothing belonging to the midshipmen and laid it on my bed. Two pairs of shoes went next. One pair was stuck in the shackles, the other pair was stuck, heels downward, into the first pair. Then two caps were stuck together for a head. The whole, being covered over with my blanket, made a very good dummy. I was highly pleased with my midnight work. The toes, sticking straight up, gave a very artistic effect to the job. Taking my hammock lashing and bundle, I went to the midshipmen's messroom.

With a stool to stand on, I took a view of the harbour from the small port-hole—about twenty inches square. These holes are open in harbour only for ventilation and light on the lower deck. At sea they must be kept closed and lashed securely. As I expected, the tide was ebbing out to sea. The ship had swung around "head on" to the city. I had no choice but to go, however. Fastening my clothes to the end of the lashing, I lowered them about eight feet, not intending to get them wet. Securing the lashing to an eyebolt, inward, I got out of the port-hole and let myself down into the water. The clothes had been dropped too low and got wet. That made them too heavy to fasten on the top of my head as I had intended. I released the bundle from the lashing, keeping it in my left hand, and then I drifted past the frigate's stern with the tide. In a few minutes I commenced swimming at an angle from the frigate, and then headed for the city. After a long swim I began to get tired and was breathing hard from exertion. The bundle worried me, and the now swift tide became too much to contend with. I had got only a short distance past the frigate, and was convinced that I could not reach the city. Then I turned back, repassed the frigate, and headed for the southern shore. The tide, at the same time, carried me towards the entrance of the harbour. I was in hopes of getting to land before I should be carried past the Sugar Loaf. As a last recourse I could let the clothing go, and that I would not do until it became a necessity. As I was swimming at an angle with the tide, not so much exertion was needed. Much to my relief I saw the dim outline of a vessel to my left. I then swam with the tide, and in a few minutes I was holding on the anchor-chain. I had a good rest and, at the same time, thought what was best for me to do. I could easily get on board at the bow, but if it were an English vessel my name would be "Dennis," sure enough. I proposed to take no more chances than necessary that night. Finally I let go of the chain and drifted to the stern. There I found the vessel's boat in the water. I got the bundle into the boat and climbed in myself.

The first thing I did was to read the vessel's name. I was then satisfied that she was a Brazilian coaster. I wrung the water from my clothes and was soon dressed up. There were no oars in the boat; if there had been I would have cut the painter and sculled with a single oar for the western shore. When I felt strong enough, I climbed up the painter to the taffrail and got on deck. No one was to be seen, so I commenced an investigation. She was a brig. On each side of the quarter-deck was a cubby-hole—a small white house with sliding-doors, just large enough for a man to sleep in. The starboard one was empty, so I knew the captain was on shore. In the port side was the mate, asleep. The cool night wind blowing on my clothes made me quite chilly. Not having decided exactly what to do, I was standing by the wheel making up my mind. A crisis was at hand. The mate crawled out of his hole, about half awake, rubbing his eyes. He caught a glimpse of me, all dressed in white, standing close to the wheel. Before I could say a word he gave a terrible yell; then he stuttered out, "Por Dios, que es esta?"—"For God's sake, what is that?" Staggering back a few steps, he turned around and ran forward, disappearing down the forecastle scuttle. Then I went to the taffrail and got the boat's painter ready for being cast off in an instant;

taking my knife from my neck, I opened it and fastened the lanyard around my right wrist. If there was to be a hostile reception, I intended to cast the boat loose and jump overboard. With the wind and strong tide, I would land somewhere, even if I had no oars. So I waited for developments. In a few minutes five men came out of the forecastle. They came aft in single file, the cook at the head with a lighted candle in his hand, the mate bringing up the rear. Then, in spite of myself, I had to laugh. It was the only time in my life at sea that I ever saw a candle on ship's deck. There are two articles which an old-time salt-water sailor has the most supreme contempt for—namely, a lantern and an umbrella. When they got close to me they were a surprised lot of men. By way of introduction, I said, "Yo soy un saltador Inglés"—"I am an English deserter." They all commenced to laugh at the mate. We soon became quite friendly, all hands considering the whole affair as a good joke. Opening the cabin skylight, they told me to get in and have a good sleep. The vessel was loaded with mahogany timber. The cabin bulkheads had been taken out and the lumber loaded through the stern ports, completely filling the brig from stem to stern. The extra sails were put in the skylight on top of the cargo. That was my bed, and a good sleep I had, even if my clothes were wet.

About seven o'clock they woke me and gave me a breakfast. I exchanged all my neat clothes with them, I getting a ragged blue jumper and overalls and a ship hat with the rim all frayed out. My shoes, stockings, and knife I retained for my own use. The boat had been hauled alongside and loaded with firewood to be taken ashore. When ready I got into it, and, taking an oar, helped row for shore. The mate gave me a friendly parting and wished me success. I thanked him, and said: "Cuidado por los brujos!"—"Look out for ghosts!" When close to shore I asked to be landed on the beach, as it would not do for me to go near the Government dock. They pulled close to a ledge of rocks and I jumped out and thanked them for their kindness. Away I went for the railroad track.

Having heard that English contractors were building a new branch, it was my intention to offer them my valuable services. I started down the track quite lively and independent. The sun became very warm and my feet sore. Then I got tired of continually looking at the telegraph-poles, each one being numbered, like houses in a city. What the reason for that was I never found out. Every station I came to I was ordered off the track, but the explanation that I was to work on the road was satisfactory. To my inquiries as to how far the new road was situated, the answer was always the same, "A few leagues farther." My five milreis now came into requisition. Some time in the afternoon I went into a general store and purchased a glass of wine, some crackers and cheese. After my feast was over, I continued my journey. Soon I had come among the coffee plantations. They looked like large cherry orchards with the trees full of ripe fruit. Two coffee grains flat side together, surrounded by a spongy fibre, then a tough, smooth skin, the whole about the size of a large cherry—that is the coffee bean while on the tree.

I do not know how many miles I walked on the Terro Carril de Dom Pedro III, but I was well tired out, and my head dizzy, from looking at the numbers on the telegraph-poles. The same information—"A few leagues farther on"—was becoming monotonous. Four milreis had been expended for food. With but one milreis left I was getting discouraged. Suddenly I changed my mind, and turned back for Rio de Janeiro. At the first station I was ordered off the track. Then I had to walk on the wagon road. One evening, about dusk, I arrived at the city, tired, hungry, and footsore. Two "dumps"—large copper coins worth forty reis each—was the last of my money. I invested one dump for a piece of cocoanut, the other for bread. That was the last food I ever ate on Brazilian soil. I had often heard sailors joking about "Mahogany Hotel-on-the-Beach," and there I went for a night's lodging. A large pile of mahogany timber hewed square for shipping, some pieces being several feet shorter than others, would make a space large enough for a man to sleep in. No doubt but that it was a very valuable edifice, but, at the same time, very uncomfortable. My apartment was about eight feet in length and only twenty inches in height and width. Early in the morning I was out of bed, with no money nor breakfast, hardly knowing what to do. There was only one thing to be done, that was to get on some vessel and get away from the city. While walking around the docks, I met the "runner" from Portuguese Joe's boarding-house. He was an American. I tried to avoid him, but it was useless. He had seen and recognised me.

"Halloa, how long have you been ashore?" he asked.

"Oh, quite a long time," I replied.

"See here, Murray, I know all about your deserting. Come down to the house and stay until we can get you away."

No, I would not take any chances in a boarding-house.

"You want to ship, don't you? Come with me and I will put you on a vessel right off."

"How much in advance?"

"Eighteen dollars," he answered.

Then I told him how I was fixed, and also that he could ship me and keep all the advance money for his trouble.

CHAPTER X
THE SPORT OF THE WAVES

WE at once went to the vessel. The captain, after asking a few questions, took us into the cabin, and I signed the articles for a voyage to Richmond, Va., as an able seaman, at fifteen dollars a month. I was then given an advance note for eighteen dollars, which I handed to the runner. I felt perfectly safe then, knowing that the note was not payable until just forty-eight hours after the vessel left port. That fact would prevent him from giving me up for the reward from the frigate. My new vessel was a swift-sailing American clipper bark—the name I have forgotten. The slaves were bringing large bags of coffee on their backs and dropping them on deck. In a couple of days the cargo was completed. There being a fair wind, the topsails were hoisted and sheeted borne alongside the dock. The lines to the dock were cast off, and our voyage to the United States began. I was aloft, loosing the main royal, as we passed close by the old Madagascar. I took off my old straw hat and waved it at the men on deck as they watched the Yankee clipper go past. I was perfectly safe then. Within an hour we had passed the Sugar Loaf. That was the last time in my life that I was to see the beautiful harbour of Rio de Janeiro.

What a contrast between the bark and the brig Grenfalls! It was child's play to steer now. A slight movement of the wheel would keep the vessel on the course. We had dry quarters on deck, fine weather, and plenty of good food and water. The only thing unusual that occurred was the large number of flying-fish that dropped on deck during the night-time. As many as fifty would be found in the morning. They are about the size of fresh-water herring. While flying they appear like streaks of bright silver. The flight is only for a short distance, however. As soon as their wings become dry they drop at once. The dolphins are their greatest enemy. In the equatorial regions, or "doldrums," as it is called, we had the usual experience—the sea as smooth as glass, no air stirring except in "cat's-paws" and coming from different directions. As soon as the little ripples would be seen on the water, the back yards would have to be braced in the proper direction to take advantage of what little wind was coming. Day after day it was the same. At last we got a steady wind and were soon on the American coast. Being in north latitude, the days were rapidly becoming shorter and the weather very cold and stormy. I suffered very much from the want of warm clothing. A shirt and pair of drawers had been given me by a shipmate. Those and the suits I had changed for with the Brazilians were all that I then possessed. The latter part of December we arrived at Richmond. I was paid off, seven dollars and fifty cents being the amount due me. A cheap suit of clothes was bought with that money, and I was again in a strange city "dead broke." I had one consolation, however, in knowing that I had quit being proxy for Mike Murray.

The large schooner Onrust was in the canal at Richmond loaded with cement for Fort Taylor at Key West and the fort on the Dry Tortugas Island. My late shipmates and myself shipped on her by the month, she being a coasting vessel. It was a novel experience for us all to be on a schooner. Everything was so different from a square-rigged ship. The captain was also the owner. Economy was his motto. Instead of eating in the forecastle, we had our meals in the cabin, the captain acting as host. None of the crew felt as comfortable as if feeding in sailor style and all etiquette dispensed with. In the forecastle was a small box stove, and that was a nuisance. The watch below would make a wood fire and go to sleep. It would only be a short time before the fire would be out and then we would wake up shivering with the cold atmosphere. As yet I did not enjoy the luxury of a bed or blankets. My finances, since leaving the frigate, had been at a low point. Besides the trouble below, we felt the cold more severely when on deck. All hands agreed on one point—that the stove was a nuisance. That was my only experience with a fire in the forecastle during my life on the sea. No matter how cold the weather, clothing wet or dry, a sailor never catches cold on the ocean if he will keep away from a stove. We sailed, instead of being towed, down the James River. When near Fortress Monroe, the main boom snapped short off near the jaws. Then there was trouble. We put into Norfolk for a new boom. Everything being ready, we hoisted sail for a new start. And such a job to get the main and foresails up on that brute of a schooner! But our experience was yet to come. In a few days we were rounding Cape Hatteras and a heavy gale came up. Then was the time the schooner showed what she could do. The main-sail had to be lowered for reefing. The hour was about midnight, and a dark, stormy winter night it was. The captain was steering, as all the men were needed for reefing, the cook included.

The first thing the Onrust did was to fall off into the trough of the sea, and in the Gulf Stream, where we were at the time, the waves were mighty lively. Then over the rails came the water and swashed around the decks, knee deep. The cook had a nice lot of firewood neatly piled up handy for use. That was travelling around in all directions, the objective point being the sailors' shins. Suddenly the main boom got loose and swung from one quarter to the other. It was "thump, thump," and sparks of fire the size of a baseball were flying over our worthy captain's head. The sheet blocks worked on heavy iron travellers, and every roll of the schooner swung the heavy boom with terrific force. All we could do was to look on and wait for the captain to get his craft head on to the sea. Bang went the boom. It had snapped short off near the jaws. Now both ends were loose, and affairs were becoming unpleasant for us "square-rigged" sailors. The heavy cargo of cement was much below the water-line, and there being no yards or heavy rigging aloft to counterbalance it, made the schooner roll extra quick and lively. The boom was very long and about fourteen inches in diameter. How it did rattle over the top of the cabin! At last, with the use of ropes, we managed to secure it. The main-sail, in the meantime, had been having its share of the fun, much to our discomfort. A storm-sail was brought from below and set. As that needed no boom or gaff, we had but little trouble to get the schooner under control again. Next in order was to save the main-sail. About fifty knots that fastened the sail had to be untied, and they being wet, made the knots hard to loosen. The boom was lying diagonally, partly on the cabin and over the port quarter. There was a narrow passageway between the cabin and the bulwarks. I was in the passageway at work, with my head between the top edge of the cabin and the boom. In trying to unfasten a foot stop I poked my head a little too far. When the next roll came the boom moved just enough to give my head a most unmerciful squeeze. I saw more stars to the square inch than could be seen with the Lick telescope! The pain actually lifted me off my feet from the deck. When the boom rolled back, I dropped to the deck all in a heap. Had the boom moved one half inch farther, my skull would have been crushed. I have had many narrow escapes from death since, but that night occurred the closest call of all. When the gale abated, the boom was taken on deck and spliced and then placed in position again. The captain was the chief carpenter.

In a short time we were in warm latitudes, and well pleased to get away from a northern winter. Passing through the Florida Keys, everything was delightful and interesting. The water was very clear. In calm weather the ocean's bottom could be plainly seen at twenty fathoms' depth. White coral was everywhere—the islands formed of it. It was the coral that made the water so transparent. On our arrival at Key West, part of the cement was landed at Fort Taylor. Then we sailed for the Dry Tortugas and landed the balance. The latter place was only a small island. Nothing but broken coral and shells were to be seen. The fort was built of brick, and about one third completed at that time. Little fishing smacks kept the place supplied with fish and green turtles. That was the first time that I saw the red snapper. It is a beautiful large fish, and excellent eating. Several wrecking schooners were in the harbour. The crews seemed to have a fine time. Their pay was a certain share of what was taken from the numerous wrecks. Piracy and wrecking meant almost the same thing in those days. One of the wreckers and myself wished to exchange places, but my captain would not consent. The schooners were about fifty or sixty tons burthen, with fourteen to twenty men for a crew. Our vessel was about five hundred men for a ton and only four men for a crew. Our main boom was larger than any mast in their whole fleet. To hoist sail for them was only child's play. With us it was a big job.

On leaving Tortugas we sailed for Mobile, Ala. On our arrival in port I severed connections with the Onrust, at the same time making a vow that if ever I shipped on a fore-and-after again, it would be a smaller craft. I went to a sailor boarding-house, and remained on shore for three weeks. Then I shipped on the C. C. Duncan for Liverpool, England. Eighteen dollars per month was the pay, and thirty-six dollars in advance. It was a fine, large American ship, a thousand tons burthen. The owners were the banking firm of Duncan, Sherman & Co., No. 17 Wall Street, New York City. The crew was composed of Swedes and Norwegians, excepting three young Americans and myself. I was the only sailor shipped in Mobile, the rest having been on board for a number of months. To show the difference in cargoes, I will describe the loading of this ship with cotton. In the first place, a hundred tons of stone ballast had to be placed in the bottom. The bales of cotton at the warehouse were put under powerful steam presses and reduced to one half the original size. The old bands were tightened with levers, and two extra bands added. Then the bale was sent to the ship and stowed as closely as possible; then jack-screws were used, and a space made for an extra bale to be jammed in, and, tier by tier, the cotton was screwed in by men who made that work a specialty. Their pay was from three to five dollars a day, with board included. The cargo was a solid, compact mass. The bales averaged about five hundred pounds each, and yet, with that heavy weight, the ship would not stand full sail in a moderate breeze. About two weeks after leaving Mobile we had a severe gale. While close reefing the main top-sail, one of the seamen was pulled over forward of the yard by the sail, and instantly killed as he struck the deck.

On that trip we saw a vessel, about two miles to windward of us, struck by a heavy squall. Its light sails were quickly furled, and the top-sails lowered. All preparations were made on our ship to do the same. We waited quite a while, but no squall came. Not a rope had to be let go. The wind must have shot high up in the clouds and passed over us. About six weeks after leaving Mobile we arrived off Holyhead. There a large tug-boat took us in tow, and we were soon going up the Mersey River, and at anchor, waiting for high tide in order to go into dock. While coming up the river we were boarded by the custom-house officers. All hands were ordered to bring out their tobacco. Then the search of the ship began in earnest. With long, sharp-pointed steel wires they prodded into everything and every place where tobacco could be hidden. It was understood that what could be found would be confiscated. Much to their disgust, none was found. What the officers had in the cabin was put into a state-room, and the door fastened with the custom-house seal.

This was my first trip to England. I'd had a good description of Liverpool from sailors, and yet I was surprised at what was to be seen. Each dock is an immense large basin, built of solid stone masonry, with large store-houses surrounding it, the whole being inside of a high wall, a large gate opening into the city. Policemen and custom-house officers patrol it day and night. Nothing can pass without examination. The tide from the sea rises from twenty to twenty-eight feet in twenty-four hours. At high tide the gates, like a lock in a canal, are opened. The ships are then allowed to enter or go out. Within a half hour the tide commences to lower, then the gates are closed until the next high water. Everything was made ready on the ship for going into dock. A tugboat had us near the gate waiting for our chance. Once inside, we had no trouble securing the ship alongside the dock. Our big anchors had to be taken on deck, that being one of the dock regulations. By evening everything was in first-class shape and very little work left to be done by us in port. After supper we all started to see the city sights by night. I was the only stranger, the others having been there before. The three Americans and myself had a very pleasant time and returned on board the vessel about twelve o'clock. Before we had undressed for bed we heard a heavy splash in the water from the forward part of the vessel, then some one from another vessel sung out, "Man overboard!" We ran to the top-gallant forecastle and could plainly see the bubbles rising in the water, but the man never came to the surface. Grappling-hooks were sent for and the body was soon recovered. One of the crew, a Norwegian, had gone to sleep on a coil of rope on the forecastle and rolled overboard. The next morning, through superstition, the crew all left the ship. We four Americans, of all the crew, alone remained. The stevedore and his gang came on board to discharge the cargo. I was anxious to see the first bale of cotton taken out. I had seen how tightly it had been jammed in at Mobile. With tackle and hooks and plenty of hard work, it was slowly pulled out. It took over a week to discharge the entire cargo. I had bought a straw mattress in Mobile, and, as it was not very comfortable, I emptied the tick and filled it with cotton. That same day a young fellow came on board and asked me if I had a cotton mattress that I would sell him. I told him I had one, but needed it to sleep on. Finally a bargain was made—he wanted the cotton only to sell. I was to receive a half-crown—sixty cents—and get the tick back. I went to the dock gate with him and told the custom-house officer that I was sending my bed to a boarding-house. The next day the bed was sold again, and I continued the operation as long as there was any loose cotton lying about the vessel. A half-crown in England was considered quite a big pile of money. For two crowns a coat, pantaloons, and vest could be purchased in those days. Our ship was chartered by the

French Government to take a cargo of coal from Cardiff, Wales, and deliver it at Algiers, Africa. A few English navvies were hired to assist working the ship. Then a powerful tug-boat took us out of the dock and towed us around to Cardiff. After getting in the dock, the navvies were sent back on the tug. There was only one dock, very wide and long, without any walls around it. It was the private property of the Marquis of Bute, a kid about five years old then. He owned nearly the whole city—it was "Bute" road, "Bute" dock, "Bute" Castle, and "Bute" everything else. We had to wait a number of days for our turn to go under the chutes. At last we commenced loading. The lower hold was about two thirds filled, the balance of the load going on "between decks," so as to leave part of the weight above the water-line. A full complement of men was shipped and we were off for the Mediterranean Sea.

CHAPTER XI
A GLIMPSE OF THE MEDITERRANEAN

SAILING south, we arrived at the Straits of Gibraltar. The wind was dead ahead. A strong current was running in from the Atlantic Ocean and we managed to beat in past the Rock after tacking ship many times. All hands were well tired out from bracing around the yards so often. On one tack we would be headed for Spain, on the other it would be for Morocco. During the night the wind died away. At daylight we found our ship was rapidly drifting on to the rocky coast of Morocco. There was not a bit of air stirring and the sea was as smooth as glass. Captain Otis was very much discouraged, as the loss of so fine a vessel meant ruined prospects for the future. He was quite a young man for such a responsible position. The Moors on the shore had seen our danger and spread the news to one another. Soon quite a number of small boats were seen at the place where the ship would probably strike. It made all hands feel a little nervous to see the reception which was awaiting us. It was well known by sailors what a set of cutthroats the people were in that locality. The officers and crew held a consultation as to what should be done. My suggestion was acted upon, and that was, to take all our boats and tow the ship, if possible, or at least to check her from drifting, in hopes that a breeze might spring up. Strangely enough, I was the only man on the ship who had ever seen the experiment tried. The occasion took place when I was in the bushes at San Carlos watching my old ship, the Courier, leaving the harbour. The wind having died away, they lowered the boats and towed the ship a considerable distance. But then the Courier was only half our size and had more and better boats than we had. Our boats were quickly lowered and fastened in a row to a rope from the ship's bows. By hard pulling we slowly turned the vessel head to the current. The drifting was checked, and that was about all we could do. Within half an hour a breeze sprang up and away started the ship, swinging the boats around and towing them stern first. We had a lively time in preventing them from capsizing when the towing business was reversed.

In a few days we sighted what appeared to be an immense hill of chalk, perfectly white from the water's edge to the summit. That was Algiers. Before night we were inside the breakwater and at anchor. That was the most interesting port I ever saw. A large number of French troops were stationed in the city. The Italian war was then in progress. Such a contrast in people and dress was probably never seen before. Only the Algerian and Moorish women seemed to be without gaiety. They were all dressed alike, a light gauzy dress and a long veil of the same material covering the head and face, leaving only the eyes uncovered. The rich wore shoes; the poor went barefooted. The young had smooth skins on their wrists; the old were wrinkled. That was the only way we could tell the difference between them. As to their beauty, we had no means of judging. Other women were dressed in silk tights and gaily coloured velvet jackets, the front being completely covered with jewels. In fact, every conceivable sort of costume was to be seen. The streets were always crowded; nobody seemed to be at home. The French soldiers were in their element, all wearing their side-arms. One regiment of Turcos looked fierce enough to annihilate a whole army. At nine in the evening, an entire drum corps would double through the town beating tattoo. Then the soldiers would disappear for the night. Wine was only eight cents a quart bottle, so their dissipation did not cost them much, especially as they did not get drunk. But how they could talk and get excited! An Englishman with such an opportunity would drink more and talk less. Most of our crew had a fondness for eau de vie—"water of life"—a cheap brandy that cost us only fifteen cents a quart. Café royale was also a favourite beverage with them—a cup of strong black coffee with brandy, the latter being bought separate in a bottle. The coffee could be doctored to any degree of strength. At first, my shipmates would take one portion of brandy, a swallow of café royale, and in would go another, and so it continued until each bottle was emptied. When ready to pay the waiter, he would count the marks on the bottle at so much a mark. There was no chance to dispute the bill, and no opportunity for the waiter to defraud the boss. I was continually eating grapes—great large bunches weighing two or three pounds each; they were white and seedless, and only two cents a bunch. Algiers was once the great stronghold of the Algerian pirates. They and the Moors laid a heavy tribute on vessels of all nations that came within their clutches. The United States sent a fleet of men-o'-war into their ports, destroyed their vessels, and liberated a number of American seamen they held in captivity. The city is built on the side of a very high and steep hill; the streets running parallel with the harbour are level, but cross streets leading up are one continuous flight of steps. You can go into a house on one street and descend from one basement to another and find yourself on the top floor of a house on another street. That cannot be done in any other city. Some of the old streets are only six feet wide, the doors in the houses being very heavy and studded thickly with large iron bolts. The windows are high from the ground and only twenty inches square, with heavy iron bars, the whole place resembling a strong prison. The new part of the city is quite modern in construction. The French introduced new ideas when they captured the country.

The French Government took the coal from our vessel as they needed it. They were paying one hundred dollars a day for the time the ship was detained in the harbour. One day I was sitting on the edge of the fore-hatch, cleaning a brace-block, when suddenly my work ceased, and I was laid up for a week. A man was aloft, tightening the truss bolts on the foretop-sail yard. He had a small iron bar which he was using at the work. Contrary to all rules, he neglected to fasten it with a lanyard. He had difficulty in turning the bolt with his hands, so he reversed the operation by holding to the rigging with both hands and pushing the iron bar with his feet. It was a success, so far as he was concerned. The bolt went around, the bar slipped out, and, whirling through the air, fetched me a whack on the side of the head. The mate gave him a good cursing for his carelessness. I was picked up, my head dressed, and was nicely tucked away in my little bed. In about ten weeks' time the coal was all discharged, the ship cleaned up, and one hundred tons of stone ballast taken on board. We left Algiers, and commenced our voyage for New Orleans. We had pleasant weather while in the Mediterranean Sea. A couple of days after leaving port, a large Swedish sailor and myself were taken sick—headache and fever—then pustules commenced to appear on our faces and hands. We all knew what that meant. It was smallpox. At first the captain intended to put us in the lower hold, but, as our vaccination marks showed very plainly, he waited for further developments. The fresh sea air and plain style of living were in our favour; varioloid was all the disease amounted to. The rest of the crew were a badly scared lot of men for a few days.

We sighted the Rock of Gibraltar, and were soon in the Straits, with a fair wind driving us strong against the current. About three miles more and we should be on the Atlantic Ocean. Suddenly the wind shifted dead ahead. All we could do then was to go back and lie behind the Rock. All sails were furled except the top-sails, and the ship hove to by backing the main yards. We made several more unsuccessful attempts. The current and wind were too much for us. We had a fine view of the Rock of Gibraltar. The western side sloped very steeply to the bay. The eastern part was perpendicular and inaccessible. A narrow, sandy strip of land connected it with Spain. England, having possession of that fortification, was there, like a big bulldog taking charge of the entrance to a house against the occupant's will. For over a hundred years the Spanish have been humiliated by their British guests. The Rock commands the entrance to the Mediterranean, and is considered impregnable. Improvements are being continually made. The galleries are tunnelled through solid rock. The magazines, bomb-proofs, and casemates cannot be penetrated by an enemy's shot. The upper guns can fire a plunging shot on a ship's deck, but a ship cannot elevate its guns enough to return the fire. The English can fire rifle bullets into Spain. With the heavy guns they can drop shot and shell into Morocco and into the Spanish forts, and, at the same time, throw tons of shot the whole length of the Straits. As there are at present, in 1897, just that number of guns in position, an enemy's fleet would receive a very warm reception. An extra gun is mounted every year. By looking on the front cover of an almanac, anybody can find out just how many cannon are mounted on the Rock of Gibraltar. About the tenth day we got a fair wind that took us through the Straits and into the Atlantic Ocean. The ship was then headed southwest for the Gulf of Mexico. In six weeks' time we sighted the lighthouse, and then the low sandy beach at the mouths of the Mississippi River. A tugboat took us over the bar, and we let go the anchor. When a tow of six vessels was obtained, a large tug towed us up the river, each ship being fastened to the other with large hawsers, stem and stern. It was a powerful boat to tow so many ships against the strong current of the Mississippi. One man was at the wheel to keep the ship straight after the tug, and all the rest of the crew were hard at work unbending the sails and lowering them on deck. The third night, about ten o'clock, we arrived at New Orleans. The ship was secured to the levee, and the voyage on the C. C. Duncan was ended.

A number of boarding-house runners came on board. Each one, of course, was working for the "best house." It was two o'clock in the morning when our work was finished. Then all the crew went ashore to enjoy a sleep on dry land. Captain Otis tried to induce us four Americans to remain on the ship for another voyage. I gave him my reasons for leaving, as it was my intention to return to my home from which I had been absent so long. I received eighty-five dollars pay that was due me, and went by steamboat to Mobile, Ala.

CHAPTER XII
IN AMERICAN WATERS

ON my arrival in Mobile, I went to work on a barge and received forty-five dollars a month. We would be towed down the bay with a load of cotton and back to the city with general freight. Ships drawing over twelve feet of water could not go up the river, consequently they had to receive and discharge in the lower bay, thirty-five miles from the city. I was on the barge for two months and then shipped on the schooner Pennsylvania, at thirty-five dollars a month. For a few weeks we brought salt to the city from the ships in the bay. Then my wages were reduced to eighteen dollars a month, as we were to take a cargo of pine lumber to Havana, Cuba. The schooner was towed up the Alabama River to a new sawmill.

During the daytime we would load timber and at night all hands would go 'possum-hunting. A few pine-knots for torches and a couple of dogs were all that was required for the sport. As soon as a 'possum was caught he would be as dead as a door-nail, to all appearances. They were put in a bag as fast as captured. On returning to the schooner, we dumped them all into an empty barrel. In the morning they would be as lively as crickets. When the barrel was hit hard with a stick, the whole lot would pretend to die a most tragic death.

When the schooner was loaded, we sailed for Havana. On our arrival in that port, the lumber was discharged. The captain, as a speculation, bought a car of oranges and bananas. The fruit was perfectly green when brought on board. We immediately set sail for Mobile. Much to the captain's disgust, the trip was a long one of calms and head winds and great trouble. The weather was intensely warm. The oranges ripened very quickly and then rapidly decayed. The fruit venture proved very unprofitable. On our arrival in Mobile, only the bananas were fit for sale. We had a nice job to clean the rotten oranges from the hold. I never see a mouldy orange but that my memory goes back to that remarkable trip.

We were towed up to the sawmill for another load of lumber. 'Possum-hunting occurred at nights as before. One of the sailors and myself wanted a pet to take to sea with us. So we went on shore on an expedition by ourselves. We at last found a big "razor-back" sow with a litter of pigs. Each of us decided that two little pigs were just the thing needed on the schooner. Then the fun commenced. "Scotty" and myself learned the fact that the pigs could do some good sprinting when there was occasion for it, and just then was one of the occasions. For a half hour we tried all sorts of tactics. It was of no use. What the little pigs didn't know the old sow did. At last we came to a big saw-log close to a fence. I was to stand at the end of the log while "Scotty" was to drive the pig family between. Everything worked nicely. I did not interfere with the sow. Making a grab, I got one pig and was laying for another. Just then there was a sudden change in the program. The old sow was doing the chasing act. "Scotty" and I did not want any more pigs! One was enough. It was "nip and tuck" as to who would win. Scotty got a stick and was pounding the sow as a diversion. I made tracks for the schooner. When I got on board I was nearly played out. The captain took a look at the pig and myself. Then he wanted to know why I didn't get a larger one while I was about it. When loaded, we sailed again for Havana. We had a pleasant trip. The schooner was small and very easy to handle. Captain Turner was a stout and short middle-aged man, very good-natured, and inclined to be tricky in regard to making money. We could draw our wages at any time we wished to do so. We arrived in Havana in the month of June. The weather was very hot. Every day at two o'clock we stopped discharging lumber, as the custom-house officers would then go home. Every board and stick of timber had to be measured on the dock. The crew would go ashore and visit the different places in the city. We all invested money in the Royal Lottery, but drew no prizes. The tickets were sold on the streets by venders, who received a commission on their sales. A person who could not understand Spanish would suppose that they were selling newspapers. The tickets were in large sheets, sixteen dollars for a whole and proportionately, down to a sixteenth.

A large American ship arrived in harbour from China with a load of coolies for the Cuban plantations. The captain was sick, so he made arrangements with Captain Turner to take his vessel, the Messenger, to New York. Our mate was to take the schooner to Boston, with a cargo of sugar and molasses. We took our cargo on board, boxes of sugar in the hold and hogsheads of molasses for a deck load. I was now going home in earnest. I purchased a lot of guava jelly and tropical preserves, besides a number of presents for my relatives. I wrote to my mother, in New York, telling her of my intentions, giving her the name of the schooner and its port of destination. The fourth day of July, 1860, early in the morning, we sailed out past Morro Castle. Our voyage to Boston had begun. I felt happy with the prospect of soon being back home. We had a very easy time on the schooner, there being nothing to do except to take our turns at steering. On a full-rigged ship it would have been different, as it is invariably the practice to keep the crew continually at work most of the time, most usually aloft, repairing the rigging. We had passed the most dangerous part of our trip, through the Florida Keys; the wind was "wing and wing"—that is, the foresail was out on one side and the main-sail on the other. A good strong breeze was driving us north at a rapid rate. That night it was my turn at the wheel from ten to twelve o'clock. It being cloudy, no stars were visible. For that reason it was more difficult to steer straight. By selecting a bright star ahead when the vessel is on the right course, it is easier to see which way the wheel is to be turned. Steering by compass alone, the vessel either "goes off" or "comes up" considerably before the compass shows it. The main boom was out to starboard the full length of the sheet. A pennant—heavy rope—from the end of the boom was hooked to a tackle and fastened forward in order to prevent the boom from swinging back. I had been at the wheel about an hour, and was watching the compass carefully. Suddenly the light in the binnacle went out. Then I had neither stars nor compass to steer by. As we were going dead before the wind, I tried to keep the old schooner straight, but it was useless. In a few minutes she yawed to starboard, and the main-sail was taken aback. All the strain of that big sail was then on the boom pennant and tackle leading forward. Before anything could be done to relieve us from our dilemma there was a sharp snap forward. The belaying-pin which held the tackle had broken, the boom flew over to the other side, and the sheet tautened out like a bow-string. It took hardly a second for the sail to jibe over.

I was lying on deck badly stunned, the wheel-post broken short off, and the wheel broken into small pieces. The old Pennsylvania was sailing in all directions. The "sheet" may be better understood by calling it a large double tackle. As the boom swung in, the sheet, of course, slackened up, and the bights, going over the quarter-deck, had caught everything in the way. If I had been caught under the arm or chin I should have been hurled quite a distance from the schooner without any possible chance of being rescued. Small tackles were fastened to the tiller, and the schooner brought head to wind. The main-sail was then lowered and furled. With only the forward sails set and all hands at the tiller tackles, we managed to run before the wind on our right course until daylight. The fragments of the wheel were picked up and, by using a stout barrel-head as a foundation, it was reconstructed. While not being a first-class affair, it answered all purposes. On the right side of my body, from ankle to top of my head, I was sore for several days. That was my second accident with main-booms, and both were narrow escapes.

Within a short distance of Boston, our stock of provisions ran short, so we had to kill our pet pig. He had grown to quite a respectable size. It was much to our regret to slaughter our companion, but it had to be done. As it was, we had nothing left to eat on our arrival in Boston. The first thing after the anchor dropped was to row the cook ashore and get some grub for supper. Captain Turner was on hand to meet us, having arrived several days previously. His first inquiries were about the pig. He intended to take it to his home. His wife had made a nice place for it in the back yard as a domicile. We went to a dock the next day for unloading cargo. A custom-house officer came on board to see that everything was according to the manifest. He was very sociable to all hands. About dinner-time he called me to one side, quietly informing me that he was going to dinner and would not return for an hour or so, and that, if the boys had anything to take ashore, they had better do it while he was absent. I told the crew what he had said. As we all had a quantity of cigars, we each chipped in a handful as a present. The balance and my supply of guava jelly was taken to a boarding-house. When the officer returned from his dinner, I told him to look on my bed. He took the hint—and the cigars too. I had to wait some time in Boston before I could get my pay which was due me, and I had not written home about my arrival, not knowing how soon I might start for New York. About the third day, while standing on the schooner deck, I noticed a neatly dressed lady coming down the dock. As it was an unusual place for a woman, my curiosity was aroused. She seemed to be looking for some vessel, so I stepped ashore and walked towards her, thinking I might be of some service to her. She was looking for her son. I was the son. It was a great surprise to me to see my mother so unexpectedly.

"Now, George, you won't get away this time; you are going straight home with me!" I was greeted.

The way she knew the Pennsylvania had arrived was by reading the New York Herald. That paper gave the daily arrival of ships in all the large ports of the United States. I told her my reasons for not writing and why I was detained in Boston; then she was satisfied. I inquired about my relations at home. They were all well and very anxious to see me. I then asked about my father in San Francisco. She at once began to cry. Then, for the first time, I noticed that she was dressed in mourning. Father had been dead just three months. I went to a hotel with mother and remained with her until evening; then she returned to New York. In a short time I received my money. The next train was taking me to New York and back to my friends from whom I had been separated for such a long time. How glad they were to see me, and what a happy time we all had! They never got tired of listening to the stories of my sailor life. I remained at home for about six weeks. As I did not wish to remain idle any longer, I concluded to return to Mobile, where I was well acquainted, and there work at discharging cargoes from vessels. I was satisfied that I could easily earn from two dollars and a half to three dollars a day at that work during the winter.

CHAPTER XIII
MY THIRD VOYAGE

ABOUT October 1, 1860, I intended to take passage on the ship Robert Ely, for Mobile, but changed my mind, for the reason that the ship had a crew of negroes instead of white men. The P. T. Bartram was almost ready to sail; the crew were all shipped, so I paid ten dollars for steerage passage, and was to furnish my own food. So many sailors wanted to go South that it was difficult for me to ship as a sailor, the boarding-house keepers having the preference with the shipping offices for their boarders. The P. T. Bartram was a bark of about six hundred tons burthen. The cargo was general merchandise—a little of everything. The North at that time furnished the Southern States with everything excepting raw cotton.

We had a fine passage to the Gulf of Mexico, with fair prospects of a speedy voyage. Slowly the fine breeze died away, the atmosphere became unusually sultry, the barometer falling rapidly. Then we knew that trouble was in store for us. It was not long in coming, either. A severe hurricane from the West Indies struck us. All sail was taken in except close-reefed main top-sail and fore-storm stay-sail. Then the bark was hove to, head to wind. The wind roared and whistled through the rigging, the waves commenced to rise rapidly and roll on deck, rain was pouring down in torrents, and lightning seemed to be striking all around us. The bark had a half deck extending to the main-mast. The after part was the cabin, the rest was for storing freight. In there were several tons of gunpowder. We did not know how soon the lightning might send us all skyward. Partly for exercise and self-preservation, I was working with the crew as one of them. The cook was with us also, since he had been washed out of the galley by a heavy sea, and would take no more chances among his pots and kettles. All hands kept aft on the vessel's quarter-deck, no other place being safe from the heavy seas. The storm kept increasing in violence, until finally the strain from the top-sails bent the main-yard up and it snapped in two. All hands started aloft to save the sails. I happened to be first, and went out to the weather side, as is customary. When about half-way out the foot of the sail, it flopped over the top-yard, struck me in the breast, and knocked me off the yard. What a queer sensation I had while falling! So many thoughts rushed through my brain in an instant, especially whether I would strike on deck or go overboard! The vessel was heavily careened over to leeward from the force of the wind, and luckily I struck in the lower rigging, my arms going between the ratlins, where I hung on for life, the pressure of the wind helping me considerably. My mishap was enough for the other men—

not one would venture on the yard. They just clung to the rigging, and let the top-sail blow away in small pieces.

With the top-sail gone, the bark fell off into the trough of the sea. Then the sea washed over the decks. For the first time on the ocean I saw the experiment tried of dragging a vessel head on to sea. The end of a large hawser was fastened to the vessel's head, the rest put overboard, in hopes that in dragging through the water the strain would swing us head on. It was not a success. The waves washed the hawser all around the bark's bow and sides. If we could have once got it straightened out, the plan might have worked. Many a shipwrecked sailor has been saved by a similar plan, when compelled to abandon a ship and take to a small boat, by fastening a rope to the middle of an oar and throwing it into the water. It has thus kept the boat's head to the seas, and prevented it from swamping. The lee-pump was kept going continually, and that was hard work. Two men at a time were at the handle. The bark was badly strained and leaking considerably. At one time we thought all the water was pumped out, but that was a mistake on our part. The pump had commenced sucking, and no water was coming up. The fact of no air hissing as usual seemed rather strange. The upper box was taken out, and then an iron hook lowered down for the lower box. When that was hauled up, the mystery was explained. About a pint of nicely water-soaked beans was holding the clapper down. By using the sounding rod, we found about fourteen inches of water below. The pump was rigged again and started, and in a few more minutes it was the same old trouble—more beans! The process of drawing the boxes was gone over again. The same result followed—more beans! A barrel of that edible fruit had broken open in the cargo, and every individual bean had found its way to the pump-well. The comments were loud and deep, and the man who invented beans was damned in all styles in several different languages.

Well, there was nothing else to do but pump the beans out on the instalment plan. Just as soon as a certain quantity got on top of the valve or clapper, it acted effectually as an automatic shut-off for the water. The hurricane had been blowing for three days and our worst danger—the terror of all sailors—was close at hand. We were drifting towards the Florida reefs. A few hours more and the ship, with all hands, would be a thing of the past. There was no possibility of escape unless the gale abated or the wind shifted to another direction. Birds by the hundreds were flying for our vessel. They were land birds of all kinds and sizes, probably blown to sea from Cuba. Striking the rigging or any part of the vessel, they would be instantly killed. Every nook and corner on the deck was filled with their dead bodies. The wind blew them around like so much dust. One was found in the compass-box, under the compass. Its presence was made known by the smell of a decaying body after the storm was over. The anchor-chain boxes had a fine assortment sandwiched in between the big iron links. Those we could not get out and, consequently, the odour was anything but pleasant in that locality. The sea had changed in colour from green to a milky white. This showed that we were getting into shoal water. The agitation of the waves was bringing up fine white coral, which formed the bottom of the ocean in the locality of the reef.

Towards sundown the hurricane had passed us, the wind gradually veering around to the north, which made a fair wind for us to Mobile. All sail was set, the damage repaired as much as possible, the cook made a lot of good strong coffee, and then all hands took turns in taking a much-needed sleep.

A remarkable sight on that trip I have forgotten to mention: one pleasant evening the sun was exactly even on the west horizon and a bright full moon on the eastern. It lasted only a few minutes, but it was a beautiful sight. All the time I have passed on the ocean, I never saw the phenomenon but that once.

The next afternoon after the storm we sighted a vessel dead ahead. On getting closer we saw a signal of distress flying. The ship had lost all her masts close to deck, was almost on her beam ends, and rolling like a log in the water. What did our gallant captain do but sail past without giving any assistance! The signal indicated that the crew wanted to abandon the wreck. All hands talked rather plainly to the captain regarding his inhumanity. His excuse was that his own vessel was too badly disabled to assist others. In a few days we were off Mobile harbour and took the pilot on board. From him we got a description of the storm at Mobile. The Robert Ely, the ship in which I had intended taking passage at first, had arrived at the beginning of the storm, and anchored outside of the harbour. The wind broke her from her anchorage and wrecked her on the low, sandy island at the entrance of the bay. Three of the crew were washed over the island into the bay on the top-gallant forecastle and rescued. The remainder were drowned.

The island had been under water. When we arrived it was completely covered with the cargo and fragments of the wreck. Pianos, boxes and barrels, all kinds of dry goods, were to be seen mixed up with the spars, rigging, and timbers of the Robert Ely. We sailed in through the channel and up the bay. As we drew only twelve feet of water we could go up the city to a wharf. A tug-boat took us in tow, and, striking a mud-bank, the good bark P. T. Bartram stuck there. Some of the cargo had to be taken out in lighters to enable us to get up the Spanish River. Much to our surprise, the dismasted wreck that we saw at sea was towed in and got up to Mobile city ahead of us.

I went ashore on board of a steamboat and, in a few hours, was back at Campbell's boarding-house, giving a description of a storm in the Gulf of Mexico. After I had finished my story, I was taken to the back yard and saw two bales of cotton which they had captured floating in the streets in front of the boarding-house. One third of the city had been under water, the upper part of a wharf had been washed away, and a flat-bottomed steamer had replaced it by standing squarely on top of the spiles. Schooners and fishing-smacks were swept into the swamp and left there—over a mile from the river. A great amount of damage had been done all along the Gulf coast.

The season was rather early for work among the shipping, consequently I was idle. Sailors were needed for a ship ready for Liverpool, but no one wanted to leave Mobile. The wages, eighteen dollars a month, remained the same, and advance pay of fifty dollars was offered and increased to one hundred, so I concluded to accept it. The trip to England would take about five weeks, and, by immediately returning, I should still have a long winter for work. The giving of nearly six months' advance pay was to evade the marine law in regard to discharging sailors in a foreign port. If sailors deserted on a vessel's arriving, the owners were not responsible. My name was signed on the articles for the full voyage. Campbell, the boarding-house keeper, got the one hundred dollars and handed my share to me. I sent part of it to New York and retained twenty dollars for myself. Bidding my acquaintances good-bye and promising to be back in ten weeks, I went by steamboat down the bay and reported for duty on the full-rigged ship Annie Size. Campbell's responsibility for the advance money then ceased. That was exactly thirty-seven years ago, and I have never seen Campbell nor Mobile since.

The Annie Size was a ship of one thousand tons burthen, loaded with cotton for the Liverpool market. The difficulty in getting a crew detained us several days. Two other men and I had made up our minds to make a short cut in the voyage. The plan was to steal the ship's boat, get ashore and foot it back to Mobile. As we had our advance money, there was no particular desire on our part to see Liverpool. The next morning, while the mates were eating breakfast, two of us got into the boat. The third man weakened and squarely "flunked." With only us two to steer as we had planned, our little scheme had to fail. The second mate had come from the cabin and had seen us going away. He called the mate, and that gentleman hailed another ship to send a boat to him. In the meantime we were doing our best to reach shore. The other boat, with a full crew, caught up with us within a few yards of the shore. We were taken back to the ship and handcuffed until the day of sailing.

Finally, the full crew was on board, and made a class of sailors that the mate had no use for. Americans, Irish, Irish Americans—men of that class usually stick together; on the other hand, a mixed crew of all nationalities does the reverse.

The anchor was weighed, our trip for Liverpool was begun, and our destination would not be reached too soon for any of us. The first day at sea war was declared. Our mate was the notorious bully, Billy Shackleford. At one o'clock he came to the forecastle door and in a gruff voice ordered watch on deck. "And he'd be ——— if there would be any afternoon watch below on his ship!" He was curtly told to "Go to ----"

"Do you fellows know who Billy Shackleford is?"

"Yes, we know all about you, and any monkey business on your part, overboard you go!"

Billy was perfectly docile for the rest of that trip. That was the toughest crew I ever sailed with—nearly all old acquaintances in Mobile. The amount of money in our possession was over a thousand dollars, in gold coin. Usually, sailors on a ship leaving port are all dead broke. An Irishman, for security, had bound a rag around his ankle containing sixty dollars. One morning his rag was missing. He bewailed his loss at a terrible rate. Somebody had quietly shaved his original style of money-belt with a razor while he was taking his sleep on deck during a night-watch. I was the next victim; twenty dollars in gold was taken from my sea chest. The chest had been opened with a key. I said very little about my loss, as I had a strong suspicion that a certain man had taken it. He had shown me how safe his money was. It was rolled up in a rag in his trousers' pocket with a string tied around the outside of the pocket, so that the money could not be reached unless the string was untied, and that could not be done without removing his trousers, as he explained to me. His custom was to get into bed all-a-stand—that is, without undressing. The first stormy night we had plenty of work to do, reefing the top-sails, and all of us were tired and sleepy when our watch went below. All were soon asleep but myself, for my hour of revenge had arrived. With a sharp penknife, I cut a slit in the trousers of my dishonest friend, the end of the pocket containing the gold slipped out, then I cut off the whole business. The money was all I wanted, and the string, rag, and remnants of the pocket I left as a souvenir.

Ten five-dollar and one two-and-a-half gold pieces was the total amount. I "planted" the money in a secure place and went to bed, and when my misguided friend awoke there was more anguish in the camp. He had my sympathy and consolation over the fact that we should both land in Liverpool dead broke, and this made our friendship more binding.

Instead of making a trip in five weeks, as we expected, we were over two months in getting to port. For a wonder, no one was killed during the voyage. The ship was towed up the Mersey River, and we arrived at Liverpool just at high tide and were taken alongside the outer dock, ready to enter the gates as soon as they were opened. Every one of us got our baggage and jumped on shore, and "dock-wallopers" had to be hired in our stead to dock the ship. Bully Billy Shackleford was furious at our leaving so abruptly, and he was politely invited to come on shore and have a parting drink, which he very wisely declined to do.

Each man had some favourite boarding-place, so we all became separated. I went to Whitechapel and had my meals and lodging at what the English call a "cook-shop." As I could not find a ship returning to Mobile, I made up my mind to go to Cardiff, Wales, by railroad, and there probably I could ship on some vessel loaded with railroad iron down to Mobile or New Orleans. My stay in Liverpool was only for two days. I crossed the river to Birkenhead—and now for my first trip on an English railroad.

On my arrival at the railroad station I purchased a ticket for Cardiff; then I wanted a check for my sea chest, but checking baggage was not a custom in England, and an official addressed me thus: "Will you 'ave your luggage booked?" My name and destination were duly inscribed. "Sixpence, please." I got on the train thinking it would be smooth sailing for "me luggage" and myself, but such was not the case. I was told to change cars at a certain station, which I did, and, at the time, I noticed that "me luggage" was on the platform at the station. Getting on my train, another link of my journey was being made, and, about nine o'clock that night, I found myself at a town called Open Gates, quite a distance on the wrong road. They informed me that I should have changed trains some distance back. "Why in —— didn't you tell me to?" was my reply. A free ride back and a new start was made in the right direction, and, finally, I brought up at a town called Newport. There the "line of rails," as they are called, ended. Twelve miles from Cardiff only, and "me luggage" and I had to take another road, and "me luggage" could not be found and no one knew anything about it. Now, what puzzles me to this day is what the "booking" meant. And I have never been able to find out, although it is the English custom. I went to a cook-shop and remained in Newport a couple of days, and in the meantime there were many inquiries about the "Young Hamerican's luggage." It was finally located, and when I changed cars the first time I learned that it was my duty to have it placed in the luggage car. While I was on my way to Open Gates, the chest was left on the platform, where I had last seen it. In the course of time a continuation of the journey was made, and at last Cardiff was reached. Hunting up an old acquaintance, he took me to a nice, quiet boarding-place.

CHAPTER XIV
PRETTY JENNIE BELL

MY friend had introduced me to the landlord's wife and the only two boarders in the house. They had resumed a four-handed game of cards. Something familiar about the landlady's face attracted my attention. "Have I not seen you before?" I asked.

"Quite likely," she replied.

Then I remembered all about her. She had been a notorious woman of the street in Liverpool. Many a time she had stopped me and my shipmates on the Bute Road and asked us to treat her. Sailors are very liberal when ashore, and very few girls are refused a drink. In England their favourite tipple is "two pen'orth o' gin and a bit o' sugar, please." The gin they drink, but the two little cubes of sugar are placed in their pockets to be eaten when there is no prospect of a free drink.

The next morning my very sociable hostess had a friendly chat with me. For old acquaintance' sake I must take her to the public-house next door and buy the gin. That place was quite respectable, but, like all public-houses in England, women would patronize it with as much freedom as men. I was simply paralyzed by an introduction I got to a very pretty young woman, by the proprietor's wife. "This is an old lover of mine, and he has come back to board with me." I was too polite to deny it, but it was an infernal lie, all the same.

I could not find a ship just then ready for Mobile. Having nothing to do, I would frequently sit in the back-room of the public-house. Everything was so cosy there! A bright fire in the grate made the room quite cheerful. The proprietor and his wife were a fine-looking and well-educated couple, always pleasant and sociable. Acquaintances were continually dropping in for a visit, and a pleasant, merry time it was for all. One of their friends was a young woman, about twenty years old, with large brown eyes, always good-natured and pleasant. She was known as Pretty Jennie Bell, and was, beyond all question, the belle of the neighbourhood. She was married, but had left her husband on account of his brutality. Nothing could be said against her character. It was then Christmas-time. I was sitting in a chair watching the fire and thinking of home. Every one in the room was laughing and looking at me. I raised up my head, and saw a branch of mistletoe held over my head. Turning around, I saw that "Pretty Jennie Bell" was the person who held it in her hand. She started to run, but I very quickly caught her, and got the kiss to which I was entitled. All the rest in the house must have a mug of beer for the kiss that I had won. Such a happy time we had that evening! Jennie and I had fallen in love with each other.

I had met an old shipmate in Cardiff, who was the first mate of an American bark. He recommended me to the captain, and I obtained the position of second mate. I felt quite proud then. It was arranged between Jennie and me that I should make a voyage, and in the meantime she would obtain a divorce; we would then get married and go to New York. Our voyage was for Matanzas, Cuba, with a cargo of coal. A couple of nights before we were to go, it was my turn to remain on the vessel. The captain and mate were on shore. As I sat in the cabin reading a book for pastime, I heard my name called. Jennie had come down to the dock alone to see me. I went ashore, and asked her if she was not afraid to come to such a dangerous place on a dark night. In an instant her arms were around my neck. "George, don't leave me," was all she said. That settled the business! I helped her on board the vessel, and took her into the cabin. We sat there talking to each other until after midnight. The mate then returned. I told him to get another second mate, as I had changed my mind about going to sea. He laughed, and bade me good-bye.

Jennie and I were both very happy then. The future was not thought about. In a couple of weeks it became very apparent that I must earn a living for my pretty wife. The fact of having no trade and being without influence to obtain suitable employment naturally made me discouraged. The English navy was giving four pounds sterling as a bounty for seamen. I shipped as an able seaman, on condition that I should be put on a man-of-war belonging to Portsmouth Harbour. My clothing and sea chest I sold. The proceeds and the bounty I gave to Jennie. I was assigned to the line-of-battle ship St. Vincent, one hundred and twenty guns. My term of service was for five years. Several other men and myself were taken across the Bristol Channel, thence by rail to Portsmouth. The St. Vincent was a very large ship, having five decks, three tiers of broadside guns, and a crew of twelve hundred men. I received some clothing and a hammock and found myself a full-fledged English man-of-war's-man for the second time in my life.

My attention was called to the bulletin offering inducements for volunteers to the Gunnery Schoolship Excellent. Men of good education, first-class seamen and physically perfect, were eligible. A man named McMinn and I made applications for the required examination. Both of us were taken on board the Excellent and most thoroughly examined. Everything being satisfactory, we were transferred and made "seamen gunners" and "submarine divers" in Her Majesty's service. The term of service was altered to twenty-one years. Extra pay was allowed for the grade of gunners. Two-pence—four cents—extra was allowed a day as submarine diver and one shilling an hour while diving, and one penny a day for each good-conduct stripe, three being the limit. A service pension was to be granted for seventeen years' service, at eight pence a day, that being additional to our regular pay. The Excellent was an old frigate anchored close to the navy yard. She had no masts or rigging, the crew having nothing more to do with the seamanship. We were divided into four divisions, each division changing exercises daily. From nine in the morning until three in the afternoon we were constantly drilling. Breech- and muzzle-loading guns, broadside guns, howitzers and muskets and rifles and pikes and cutlasses, all came in rotation, and target practice daily with big guns and small arms. Then, by turns, we would put on the submarine armour and practise at diving in thirty feet of water. On Saturdays and Sundays we had a rest. Five days' drilling in a week was sufficient. When a man-of-war was ready for sea an order would be sent to the Excellent for the same number of seamen gunners as the ship had guns. Then we would rank as Captains of the Guns and receive pay as petty officers. For instance, a frigate of forty guns was ready for sea; forty men from the Excellent would be sent on board. As soon as the frigate returned from a cruise the forty men would be sent back to continue their practice in gunnery. At three of the afternoon, every day, three divisions were at liberty to go on shore and remain until half-past seven the next morning.

I at once rented a nicely furnished room for light housekeeping for one half crown a week. Then I sent for Jennie. On her arrival, everything was made pleasant and comfortable. I would be at home three nights out of every four. Saturdays I would be at liberty at eleven o'clock in the morning until Monday morning. My wife would draw one half my pay every month, one quarter pay was given to me in cash monthly, and the other quarter I could draw in clothing and other necessaries. I needed all my pay, and it required sharp practice to get it. I could get one pound of tobacco monthly. That cost one shilling, government price. I sold it immediately for two shillings. I drew flannel, and sold it at a profit. I kept my account about square with the paymaster. As I drank no grog, tea and sugar were given me in lieu of it. McMinn and I were very friendly. He was a temperance man and gave me his allowance of tea and sugar. At the end of each month I had quite a quantity due me. My half-pay was allotted to Mrs. Jennie Thompson, Portsmouth. Then we were in a quandary. It was necessary for a wife to show a marriage certificate before she could get the money. Now that was a document that Jennie did not possess. That little obstacle did not bother us very long. We went to the Register's office and were married in orthodox style. Jennie did not worry much over the fact of committing bigamy. She got the certificate and half-pay, too. We lived together very happily. I never knew her to be ill-natured or say a cross word. I always had a cordial welcome, and a pleasant smile awaited me. What money I earned was spent to advantage. I neither drank liquor nor used tobacco. My nights were always passed at home with Jennie, and happy hours they were, too!

One night, while my division was on duty aboard the ship, we had quite a diversion from the ordinary routine. A big fire was seen on shore. All boats were "called away" and our division landed at the navy yard, each man carrying a ship's fire-bucket. A lieutenant had charge of the "fire brigade" of about one hundred and fifty sailors. Nothing pleases a sailor more than having something to do on land. Going to a fire was an unusual treat. Steam fire-engines were not invented at that time. For a New York city man that fire was a comical sight. On our arrival at the scene, we found a regiment of soldiers drawn up in double line around the burning buildings. Behind them were about all the prostitutes in the city——and they were numerous in proportion to the population. The soldiers opened ranks for us to pass inside the lines, the women encouraging the sailors by singing out, "Go it, Excellents! Be lively, my lads!" The troops had their muskets and, in their bright scarlet uniforms, made a grand display. Only one old-fashioned fire-engine, worked by hand, was to be seen. The old box was so leaky that the water was spurting in all directions except the proper one. Our gallant lieutenant, with his drawn sword pointed to the burning building, was ordering us to put out the fire. The whole block was a row of small two-story brick buildings. As one house would burn down, the next would catch fire. The fire-buckets were of leather, with a rope thirty feet in length attached to each one, for the purpose of hoisting water over the ship's side and lowering it down the hatches in case of fire. On shore the circumstances were different. The rope was a great impediment. But something must be done to show what sailors could do at a fire.

A dam of mud was made in the street gutter, the leaks in the fire-engine furnishing abundance of water. All hands were formed in line and each man, dipping up a bucketful of water, would run to the burning structure, the lieutenant with his sword would point out the particular second-story window into which he wanted the contents of the bucket thrown, and so it would go. That plan was a dismal failure. It would require men about twenty feet in height for that style of fire-fighting. The agents of the insurance company asked us to tear down a building about six houses to the leeward of the fire. By that means the fire could be checked from spreading. The fun then began in earnest. A stick of timber was used as a battering-ram for the outside; inside the building the sailors were like a swarm of bees. One enterprising man was boosted up into the attic; he did not remain there long, however, for, making a misstep, he went through the second-story ceiling, his body and a quantity of plastering landing on his shipmates below. That building was a complete wreck in a very short time.

While the wrecking was in progress, some of the sailors had got on the roof of a building next to the fire. Then the hose was pulled up, and during that process the sailors close by got a good ducking occasionally. Somehow, the sailors could not control the nozzle properly——at least they said so. In a short time the fire was put out, and there were four buildings not damaged between the ruins and the wreck. How that insurance agent did growl and rave!

All hands picked up their buckets and were marched to the navy yard, and on our way a saloon-keeper was called out of bed and the lieutenant treated each man to a pint of beer. About daylight we were on board the ship again. The sailor who so gallantly held the nozzle and squelched the fire was in luck. The insurance company made him a present of ten shillings, and also wrote a letter to the captain of the Excellent, praising the conduct of the aforesaid sailor. As he had ruined a fine pair of trousers which cost him twenty shillings to replace, his reward was considered quite small. The men in the house-wrecking business were inclined to be envious; they were not even thanked for their hard work.

By hard study and strict attention to duty, I soon became a good gunner. The cutlass exercise I was very fond of. Every evening, when I remained on board, I would get some good man to use the single sticks with me for amusement, and, consequently, I became quite a good swordsman. In April we received news in regard to the Rebellion in the United States. Jennie and I had a long conversation on the subject, and both concluded that it would be much better for me to be in the United States navy, where promotion was possible. The pay was also much better. Besides, I was not an Englishman, and it was my duty to fight for my country. It was arranged that Jennie should go home to her parents, and remain there until I could send for her from New York. I was to desert from the Excellent.

Now, deserting from that vessel was a serious affair, as neither labour nor expense was spared in capturing a deserter. The penalty was not less than one year in prison. It was very seldom that a gunner ran away, and nearly every one who did so was caught. I got a canvas bag, such as sailors use, instead of a chest. Taking it home, I filled it with any old dresses or rags that Jennie could get. I brought two No. 3 grape-shot from the ship, and put them in with the other trash. My object was to have my baggage to take with me. I told McMinn of my intentions. He had his discharge from the English merchant service, which he gave to me, as it might be very useful. My sailor clothes I sold, except the suit I had on. Jennie told our landlady that she was going home on a visit. Everything being ready, we bade each other an affectionate good-bye, and she went away. The next day I got a pass from the captain for permission to travel for twenty-four hours unmolested. I got my man-of-war's suit changed, and, taking my baggage, and getting on the cars, I was in London in a few hours.

Securing my bag, I at once went to the Sailors' Home on the East India Road, registering my name as John McMinn, also showing the discharge from the merchant service. I stated that I had been home several months on a visit. The Home was a very large building built by the Government for the protection of sailors from the numerous boarding-house sharks. The charges were just enough to cover all expenses, and each man had a small room to himself, besides the use of the library and the bathing-room. There was also a large sitting-room, and a shipping office was on the lower floor. Men could be shipped there or paid off; in fact, everything was done to protect sailors from being defrauded. Early the next morning I went to London dock. In a short time I found an English brig ready for sea. Showing my discharge to the captain, he told me that I was just the kind of man he wanted, and gave me an order to be shipped. I went to the Home and signed the Articles for a voyage to St. Kitts, West Indies.

An advance note for two pounds ten was given me, and the next day, at ten o'clock, the brig was to sail, that being the time of high tide, and the dock gates open. That also was the time that I would be proclaimed a deserter from Her Majesty's service, it now being twenty-four hours after my pass had expired. I had no intention of going to St. Kitts, and about nine o'clock I settled my bill, and, picking up my bag, was going out of the door, when I met one of the owners of the brig.

"Ah, my lad, I came to ship another man in your place. We thought you had backed out."

"Oh, no!" I replied. "I am just on my way to the docks."

"Then hurry, lad, you have no time to lose."

Well, that brig went to sea with my name on the Articles. That was what I wanted. But I was not one of the crew. I went to a shipping office, threw my bag into a corner, and told them that I wanted to ship on a vessel. I was sent to an American ship to see the mate, and from him I got an order to be shipped. The voyage was around Cape Horn to Callao, Peru, from there to Australia, and thence to the United States. That trip would be around the world and would take a year to complete.

CHAPTER XV
GOOD-BYE TO ENGLAND

MRS. MASSEY was in charge of the shipping office, and, showing her the order and saying that I would ship, I walked out, and straightway back to the dock I went. I found the vessel that I really wanted. It was the packet-ship Rhine, bound for New York with emigrants. From the mate I got an order to be shipped from a certain office. I went to Massey's for my bag, and, as I picked it up and started for the door, Mrs. Massey asked me if I had backed out, and I curtly told her that I had. Then she showed her good breeding. Such language I never heard a woman use before. "— —, — who enticed you from this office? — — —!" Two young men happened to be standing in front of the door. "— are these the men?" she asked. "Yes," I answered, and what a tongue-lashing those two fellows got! In the meantime I walked off. I found the right office and shipped for New York. I received an advance note of two pounds ten. A young man in the office offered to take me to a small boarding-house, and arriving there, I was introduced to the landlord. He was an old sailor, a native of Chile, and the fact of my having lived there made us friends at once. I made a bargain for two days' lodging, a straw mattress, sheath knife, tin pot, pan, and spoon. Besides, he was to have five shillings extra for cashing my advance note. The difference he paid me in cash. Then I went to the post-office and bought an order for every cent I had, made payable to Jennie Bell, and, remaining in the house until the sailing, I wrote a letter to Jennie, merely stating that I would be in New York four weeks from that time. The money-order was inclosed and the letter mailed just before the ship left the dock. We sailed down the Thames River into the Channel, and at sundown the white chalk cliffs of Dover were far astern. That was the last time I ever saw the coast of England.

The Rhine had a large number of steerage passengers on board. Men, women, and children were all huddled together between decks. They all got sea-sick, and it is a wonder that none of them died. The filth and stench were terrible. The crew were a tough lot, being mostly old "packet rats," as they are termed. They would stay on shore until their advance money was all spent, then they would have to ship. They would steal all of their clothing from their more provident shipmates. My bag had been searched, but it only set them wondering as to who I was, with all the old rags and the two grape-shot. In just one month's time we sighted Sandy Hook, New York. The passengers were all on deck, getting their first glimpse of America, and were all glad that the voyage was so nearly ended. The twin lighthouses of the Highlands of Navesink were in plain view; below them was a famous summer resort for New Yorkers. As I stood on that deck watching the beautiful scenery, a dirty, ragged suit of sailor's clothes on my back, not a cent of money in my pockets, had a fortune-teller then said to me—"See that hotel on the beach? One year from now you will be staying there as a guest, and paying twenty-five dollars a week for your accommodation. You will be the best-dressed young man in the house and wearing diamond jewelry, with the waiters eager to wait upon you, as you are very liberal in giving tips. And Matilda, the proprietor's daughter, will be your betrothed wife"—I should have laughed at the idea; but it all happened so in reality.

As we sailed through the Narrows it became my turn to steer the ship; the captain and pilot standing close to me conversing, I heard the pilot say that the docks were crowded with ships, and that the Rhine would have to remain anchored in the bay a week before docking. The captain replied that it would give them a good opportunity to have all the rigging tarred. Now, hearing that conversation nearly cost me my life. Tarring a ship's rigging is about the hardest work and the dirtiest job imaginable, and, besides, the hands and finger-nails are dyed a dark-brown colour which remains for weeks. None of that work for me just then! As the anchor dropped, my duty at the wheel was ended. The boarding-house keepers came alongside and were soon on deck looking for victims. A hard-looking case asked me if I had ever been in New York before.

"No, this is my first trip across the ocean."

"Well, come to my house. I have a nice place."

"All right," I answered, "I will go, on condition that you get my clothes and take me from the ship right off."

He told his runner to take his row-boat under the port bow. Going to the forecastle, I pointed out my bag. I was to go in the boat; then he was to throw me my valuable wardrobe. The passengers were at the rail, looking at Castle Garden. Crowding in between, I found there was a rope hanging over the ship's side, and, in an instant, I was on the rail, grabbing hold of the rope. I intended going down "hand over hand" with my feet on the vessel's side, but the rope was not fastened as I supposed, consequently I fell about twenty feet, striking the water back first and just barely missing the row-boat. The runner helped me in, then down came the bag, and we were off for dry land. My career on the ocean as a sailor before the mast had terminated most unexpectedly to me, and that proved to be my last voyage.

On landing, we walked to the worst locality in New York city. On the way I was told that a brig bound for the West Indies needed a crew, and would I ship on her? "Certainly," I replied. Now the intention was to "shanghai" me (that is, steal my advance money), my landlord supposing that I was a greenhorn. Finally, we entered a dirty old house on Cherry Street, the worst street in the city at that time. I was invited to take a drink, which I refused. The sleeping apartment was shown to me——a filthy room with bunks around the sides, made out of rough boards. The brig was to sail the next day.

"Well, I must have a new pair of shoes."

"All right, come with me."

He took me to a store and I selected a pair, which were charged to the landlord.

"Now I want a hair-cut and a shave."

Into a barber-shop we went, and that was also charged up. Going back to the house, I had my supper, and it was a holy terror for "shore food." I loafed around the place until after dark, then I started for home, being ashamed to have the neighbours see me in daylight in my ragged and still wet clothing. As for the sailors' boarding-house, it was only a case of "wolf eat wolf." They had simply caught the wrong man for a sucker.

I rang the door bell and a strange servant girl asked me whom I wished to see. Without answering, I walked in and opened the sitting-room door. My return was a complete surprise. One of my cousins, a young lady, cast pitiful glances at my clothing, as much as to say, "Poor fellow, he must have had a hard time!" Fortunately, on leaving home the last time, I had left my best suit of clothes behind. It was only a short time before I had a good bath and was dressed like a civilized being. We remained in the sitting-room talking until after midnight. My travels and the war were the topics of conversation. Next morning I went to the post-office and got a letter from Jennie. The detectives had traced her home and all kinds of questions were asked in regard to me. But she knew nothing. They said it made no difference, as they would have me back in England in a few weeks, for I had shipped on an English ship for St. Kitts and orders had been sent to the admiral of the station to arrest and send me back in irons at the first opportunity.

In the afternoon I went to the naval rendezvous, and passed examination as an able seaman for the United States navy. The pay was eighteen dollars a month, with chance of promotion. But there was a hitch in the proceedings. The quota of able seamen was filled, and the best I could do was to ship as an ordinary seaman at fourteen dollars a month. That I refused to do, and I explained that I was fully capable of being a petty officer, and that I would not throw away my chances for being rated as such by shipping as an ordinary seaman. I was invited to come again in a few weeks, as more men would be required, and they preferred young Americans like myself in the navy. In a few days I had made up my mind to go into the army. The companies and regiments throughout the Northern States that were being organized had to be disbanded for lack of arms and clothing, and also for the reason that the Government had no expectation of needing their services, so my patriotism was squelched for the time being. A number of my young friends had enlisted for three months, under the first call for seventy-five thousand men. They nearly all got back, and stayed home for the remainder of the war, having had all the glory they wanted.

CHAPTER XVI
WHAT MONEY CAN DO

I WROTE to Jennie, telling her that arrangements had been made for her to live with my mother for awhile, telling her also to let me know when she would be ready to leave England, as the money would then be sent to pay her expenses. In a month's time I received a very formal letter from her sister stating that, through mediation of relatives, Jennie and her first husband had become reconciled, and were again living together. I showed the letter to my mother and explained everything. She was pleased at the termination of the affair, but, somehow, she took no stock in my wife's morality. I had about concluded that my valuable services would not be needed in the war, so I went to Duncan & Sherman's banking house in Wall Street, intending to ship in one of their vessels, if possible. There I met Captain Otis, who was in command of the C. C. Duncan when I made the voyage to Algiers. He had quit going to sea, and was married to Mr. Duncan's only daughter. Through his influence, I obtained a good situation as outdoor clerk for the banking house. My work was principally about the shipping at the docks. I was delighted at the prospect of remaining at home and living on dry land. The excitement over the war had quieted down considerably in New York. Regiments passing through the city for Washington were loudly cheered and soon forgotten. In the meantime the rebels were strongly fortifying the Southern coast, and loudly proclaiming that "Cotton was King." The battle of Bull Run made it quite plain to both parties that they had a big contract on their hands. The celebrated New York Fire Zouaves did not go to Richmond as they intended. A number of them became demoralized, and never stopped running until they got back to Fulton Market, in New York.

The few ships in the navy captured Port Royal, in South Carolina. Some of the Confederates from there never stopped until they reached Canada. Then came Hatteras Inlet and Roanoke Island, N. C. The Government secured all the steamers available for the use of the navy, even taking the old Staten Island ferry-boats. Gold became very scarce and at a premium. Legal-tender notes were then issued, and Government bonds sold at a discount. For small change, postage-stamps were used. All the silver coin was being hoarded up and withdrawn from circulation. A revenue tax was placed on everything. On whisky it was two dollars a gallon. Even the poor people had to pay for the revenue-stamps on the pawn-tickets when they pledged articles. Before the war ended, good tea was two dollars and a half a pound; coffee, from forty cents to a dollar; sugar, twenty-two cents; a common round of beefsteak, twenty-five; turkey, thirty-five cents a pound, and eggs sixty cents a dozen. There was plenty of work, with high wages.

I still kept my situation and was gradually working my way up. My associates were very different from those I came in contact with while a sailor. Knowing as much as I did about the Havana Lottery, I had great faith in it. By very little persuasion, I got six young men to go in with me to co-operate in the purchase of tickets, each one paying a certain sum weekly. Every month tickets would be bought for the full amount. The bankers, Taylor & Company, in Wall Street, were the agents. For several months it was the same thing——no prizes. In the month of April, 1862, there was rejoicing in the club. We had drawn a fifty thousand-dollar prize! Taylor & Company cashed it for us at a small discount. The seven sharers received the money——a little over seven thousand dollars each. Then we all went to the devil. No use working with all that wealth, so we left our situations.

At first a silver watch costing thirty-five dollars was good enough for me, then I changed it for a gold one worth one hundred and forty. A diamond ring came next, for one hundred and twenty-five dollars. And of course I must have a diamond breastpin, one hundred and twenty-five more. I got to be very particular about the style of my clothing. A bottle of wine with my suppers was just the thing. How I did lie back and contrast the present with the past while on board a ship!

Not feeling very well, I concluded to spend a few weeks at a summer resort. My friends recommended me to Teller's Pavilion, at the Highlands, Navesink, N. J. My expenses there were quite heavy: twenty-five dollars a week for a nice room, one bottle of wine for dinner, two dollars and a half extra. To be well waited on called for liberal tips to the waiters. As my money had come easy it went easy. I made a lot of friends, and usually paid all the bills for boating parties and other amusements. I became acquainted with Miss Tillie Teller, and with us it was a case of "love at first sight." Finally, we became engaged. I presented her with a fine diamond engagement ring. The season ended and I returned to New York.

Having spent a large share of my money, I concluded to start in some business with the remainder, make a good living and marry Tillie. A saloon on Broadway seemed a good investment. Well, as a saloon proprietor I was a dismal failure. It was nothing but woe and misery. Every one robbed me right and left. I got into debt, lost all my respectable friends, broke my engagement with Tillie, and married another girl; and that wife put the finishing touch on the whole business. Annie was her name. She was very pretty, with blue eyes, light hair, and petite figure. How innocent and childish in her ways! She could make me believe almost anything. I had more rows on her account than a prize-fighter could conveniently attend to. If we went on the street-cars, to the theatre, or into a restaurant, there would be trouble with some one in short order. It made no difference where we lived, it would be the same old program; the first two days all would be lovely, until she got acquainted with the neighbours, and then war would be declared. And I, like a fool, believed her to be in the right. As regards her education, it was much below the average standard. What she lacked in that respect, however, was counterbalanced by her ingenuity in inventing lies. It took a long time for me to discover her talent in that line. Her fictions were not overdone; they were simply just good enough to believe.

Becoming disgusted with the saloon business, I concluded to sell out at any price. I was in debt, head over heels, and what little money was taken in was stolen by the barkeeper. I was offered four hundred and fifty dollars for the place and accepted it. It cost me twelve hundred. I made a great mistake in not insisting upon having my little angel of a wife included in the sale, but it required a few more years' time for me to become fully acquainted with all her virtues. She certainly was a terror. As a diversion she would have a fit of hysterics. I was not well posted on that female peculiarity. At first, I was badly scared and did some lively petting and nursing. Finally, the thing became rather monotonous, so that when she felt like thumping her head against the door or bed-post, I would go to sleep and let her amuse herself to her heart's content. She recovered muck quicker, as I found out by experience. Taking a dose of laudanum was also a favourite trick, but, unfortunately, she never took an effectual one.

CHAPTER XVII
THE NEW YORK DRAFT RIOTS

I HAD sold all of my jewelry. The proceeds of the sale of the saloon were nearly all paid out for my debts. My financial affairs were in a low condition, with a loving wife to care for. What made my affairs worse was the prospect of soon becoming a father. At that time there was considerable war excitement in New York. The rebels had broken loose and had invaded Pennsylvania. All the New York State militia were then sent to the front. My mind was fully made up to enter the navy as soon as our child was born and my wife well. The grade of ensign had been created in the navy. Getting good recommendations from Duncan, Sherman & Company and from Captain Otis, I made application to the Secretary of the Navy—Gideon Welles—and received permission to be examined for the position of ensign.

The draft riots in the city had begun (July, 1863) and all business was at a standstill. The three hundred dollars' clause was the cause of the trouble. A man in moderate circumstances could pay that amount and be exempt from military service, but a poor man would be compelled to go. The State militia being away, the city was defenceless. Besides, there were thirty thousand known criminals among the population, and a great number of rebel sympathizers. The drawing of names for the draft took place at Forty-second Street and Second Avenue. Early in the morning a large mob gathered and very quickly drove the officers from the building and gutted the place most thoroughly. The police from that precinct came running up Second Avenue, and used their clubs very freely. When they got close to the mob, affairs were different. The rioters disarmed the police and gave them a most unmerciful beating, several being killed outright. One had sought refuge in a house, where he was found hidden under a mattress and thrown out of a second-story window. Everything in the building was destroyed and the place set on fire. The same result happened at every house where a policeman had been assisted or sheltered. Next the Invalid Corps, composed of disabled soldiers, made a charge on the crowd.

They were disarmed and driven back, and in a short time news of the riot spread over the city and pandemonium reigned for the time being. All places of business were closed and not a policeman dared to leave the station-houses. A number of good citizens took possession of the armories and arsenals and guarded them from capture by the rioters. Buildings in different parts of the city were set on fire, and the firemen would be on hand with their engines, but would not be allowed to throw a single stream of water. The Coloured Orphan Asylum was pillaged and burnt to the ground. The Old Firemen's was an organization that gave its services without pay, but its members were exempt from military duty. Their engines were worked by hand, the companies having from seventy-five to one hundred and twenty-five members each, and were always present at the fires, but were powerless to do anything. The mob had sense enough not to attempt to injure any of the engines, as that would have precipitated a fight with the fire laddies, and they had the reputation of being fighters from the word "Go."

Down town, the rioters made an attack on the New York Tribune building, but old Horace Greeley was prepared for war. The doors and windows were barricaded with bales of paper and behind that were all the employees, all heavily armed. The mob took in the situation and went after something that was easier, such as chasing negroes into the East and North rivers and watching them drown. At Twenty-first Street they caught several and hanged them to lamp-posts; then straw mattresses were placed under them and set on fire. United States marines were sent from the Brooklyn Navy Yard to guard the United States Treasury building on Wall Street, as well as the banks in that neighbourhood. Towards evening the rioters became drunk and more reckless; nothing could be done to check them, and all the respectable citizens anticipated a night of terror. Fortunately, about eight o'clock a heavy rain commenced to fall, and that caused the drunken brutes to disappear. The rain also extinguished the fire in the many ruins in different localities. The next day the weather was quite pleasant, and the rioters, early in the morning, recommenced their work of destruction; houses would be pillaged and then set on fire. The lower class of people, especially the women and children from the tenement-houses, could be seen carrying off everything that was portable. The thieves were very busy stealing all the valuables when a house was first raided, and they were usually the first to make a demonstration at any building, the mob being always ready to follow, on general principles. The police remained in the station-houses, not one of them daring to come outside, as it would have been certain death to do so.

Gun and hardware stores were broken into and looted of all arms and ammunitions, and, by that means, a large number of the most desperate rioters became armed. A mob composed of about five thousand men started for the Fifth Avenue Hotel, situated on Madison Square, considered at that time the finest and most aristocratic hotel in the United States. As they came close to the building, yelling loudly, "Burn the Fifth Avenue! Loot the Fifth Avenue!" all anticipating an exciting time as well as plenty of rich plunder, the whole thing was suddenly changed. The occupants of the hotel had been watching the advance of the mob—not knowing their intention—and as the rioters entered the Square, howling and hooting, every window in the building was occupied by the guests, who loudly cheered and waved handkerchiefs to show that they were in full sympathy with the mob. That ended the affair, as the rioters were not disposed to injure any of their openly avowed Copperhead friends. The cheers were returned, and no other demonstration was made. The Fifth Avenue was a regular resort for secessionists and rebel sympathizers during the war. In any other country such a place would have been closed up and all of the occupants put in prison.

Towards night a few of the militia arrived in the city, and the rioters killed a few of them by filing from the windows and house-tops in the tenement districts. The morning of the third day more troops arrived, and the mob scattered in all directions upon the approach of the soldiers, only to mass together again in another locality. In the morning a regiment of infantry marched down Second Avenue and the colonel stopped on some private business on Twenty-seventh Street, when two rioters sneaked up behind and knocked him senseless with a club. Then the crowd quickly gathered, a rope was procured, and the colonel was strung up to a lamp-post. In the meantime the regiment was marching along in complete ignorance of their colonel's fate. The body was soon cut down and dragged through the streets, receiving all kinds of ill-treatment. Rioters' wives hurled paving-stones at the prostrate body, and what was most strange was the fact of his retaining life until late in the afternoon. He was a very powerful man and must have had wonderful vitality. Near Tenth Street was a large building used as a manufactory of muskets and revolvers. The rioters had broken in and were helping themselves to everything portable, and, in fact, they were so busy that they did not know that Colonel Lynch's regiment was at hand, and when they did realize that fact it was too late, for, as they came rushing out, they were shot down without mercy. A number of them jumped out of the windows only to be killed or maimed for life as they struck the sidewalk. Quite a large number was killed by soldiers, and those who escaped spread to the different parts of the city and circulated the story that the soldiers would shoot to kill.

That night the riot was nearly ended, for more troops had arrived and the police were again on duty. The next morning the bakers, butchers, and grocers resumed business. Those people who had not a good supply of provisions on hand had a hard time while the riot lasted, as not a single article could be purchased. For three days not a street-car or vehicle of any description could be seen on the streets, nor was a coloured person, male or female, visible during the period; probably the only time in the history of New York that such conditions prevailed, for a New York negro, as a usual thing, is not very bashful about making his presence apparent to all who come in contact with him. The Southern sympathizers were actually the ones who brought on that riot, for they were always up to some mischief, and a few months afterwards assisted Dr. Blackburn to distribute clothing infected with small-pox to the poorer classes in the city, but the plot failed.

Next came the attempt to burn the whole city by starting fires simultaneously in different localities. Each of the firebugs carried a black satchel containing self-igniting chemicals, which were to be dropped on the stairways of the large buildings. Barnum's Museum was set on fire, and several other places also, with but little damage resulting, and, about that time, any one caught with a black satchel would suddenly come to grief.

My wife having recovered from her confinement, and the riot being ended, I went to the Brooklyn Navy Yard, and underwent a medical examination. Next, I was thoroughly examined in navigation and then in seamanship. Having passed in all, I was ordered to return again in a few days and, in the meantime, to provide myself with the regulation uniform. My money was all spent by that time, so I borrowed enough with which to buy my new outfit. In due time, I received my appointment as an acting ensign in the navy. The pay was thirteen hundred dollars a year. There were three classes of officers in the navy: first, the regulars; second, the volunteers, composed of officers who had resigned previously to the war; and third, the acting officers who volunteered from the merchant service. The rank and pay was the same in all classes. I was at once ordered to the St. Lawrence, for instruction in gunnery. Quite a number of ensigns and masters' mates was on board, getting initiation as to how a ship's battery should be handled. The first day's exercise was sufficient for me; I was pronounced proficient and excused from further drill. The other officers were surprised at my learning my duties so quickly, but I never mentioned my experience on the gunnery-ship Excellent.

CHAPTER XVIII
ACTING ENSIGN IN THE UNITED STATES NAVY

GENERAL CANBY, who commanded the troops in New York city, had chartered six tug-boats for patrolling the river fronts, and each one had a howitzer and guns, in charge of an ensign. I was sent to take charge of the boat Rapid, and my instructions were to remain at Castle Garden dock and await orders. As there was no more rioting, my chance for killing a few rebel sympathizers was lost. One day a young man approached me and inquired for the tug-boat Rapid, as he wished to see Ensign Thompson.

"You are speaking to him now," I answered.

He looked at me rather quizzically for a few seconds, and said his name was John Murray.

"The fact is, you are living with my wife."

"The devil I am!" I replied.

"Such is the case," he stated. "I was arrested and compelled to marry her, and, after living together for a year, she ran away from me in Canada and came to New York. Now I wish to get a divorce so that I can marry a girl to whom I am at present engaged."

At first he talked of having her arrested for bigamy. I told him that even if he did that, he would still have to get a divorce, and that a man who would ruin a girl and then contemplate sending her to prison was a contemptible cur. Finally it was arranged that the divorce notice should be served on her, and a decree asked for. My interview with Annie was rather stormy. I told her that I would not marry her again, but I would take care of her and would treat her as a wife as long as she behaved herself. That was my last matrimonial venture; and I was a man married to two women and yet legally a bachelor.

About the 1st of September, General Canby gave me orders to return the howitzer and sailors to the navy yard, also for me to report to the St. Lawrence. In a few days I was ordered to Boston, to join the United States brig Perry. On my arrival, the captain indorsed my orders as having reported. Next, I went to the navy agent, and received two hundred dollars as advance pay and my mileage expenses from New York—twenty-one dollars and ten cents. All naval officers are allowed ten cents a mile when ordered to the different naval stations. The next day I reported as ready for duty. Being next in rank to the captain, made me executive officer. The Perry was the vessel I admired so much when in Rio de Janeiro. Now the circumstances were altogether different. It was a most undesirable vessel to be attached to in war times. There would be no chance of active service or prize money. The Perry's day had passed with the advent of fast steamers for blockade-running. In the early part of the war she captured the rebel privateer Dixie after a short engagement, and that was the end of her victories. And not one cent of prize money was ever credited to her account.

The Perry was a man-of-war of the fourth rate, carrying ten broadside guns and one howitzer. She was a very fast sailer, but very cranky or top-heavy, on account of the heavy battery on deck and her lofty spars. An acting master was in command. Under him were five acting ensigns and three active master's mates. Captain (by courtesy) William D. Urann was a thorough seaman, but a mighty mean person. He was a close-fisted down-East Yankee. I was the only ensign on the brig for about a month, the master's mates acting as watch officers. At last we got four other ensigns, and every one of them was my senior, so that fact dropped me to navigating officer. The commandant of the navy yard reported to the naval department that the United States brig Perry was ready for sea. Then the trouble began. Both officers and sailors were trying all kinds of plans to get transferred to some of the steam gunboats. Some of the crew complained about the foremast being rotten. The boss carpenter was sent on board to examine it. After boring a few augur holes in it he pronounced it sound. Then the crew had other complaints about the vessel. Now, when a sailor gets to growling he can do it to perfection, and the result was that the commandant sent a number of the growlers to the receiving ship, very much to their joy. They were all good seamen. In their place we received some very useless negroes to fill our complement of men. The officers complained of being sick, and everything else they could think of, so an extra ensign was sent on board to assist us. As that gentleman was my junior by a few days, he had to be the navigator and I became a watch officer. We were to pass many a day of misery together in Southern prisons.

Very much to the commandant's relief and our own disgust, the anchor was weighed, and we set sail for Charleston, S. C. All went nicely until we got near Cape Hatteras, when, during a storm, some of the fore-rigging carried away. We all examined the parted stays, and pronounced them rotten, and the officers had quite a consultation as to what should be done under the circumstances. Finally, the captain said that if the six ensigns would go aloft and examine the rigging, and then make an individual report that the vessel was unseaworthy, he would put back for New York. We gave our report in very quickly, and the brig was headed for Sandy Hook, N. Y. On our arrival at the navy yard, when the reasons for our coming into port were made known, there was a big rumpus, sure enough. The presumption on our captain's part was simply enormous! Had not the commandant of the Boston navy yard reported the Perry as ready for sea? All the officers on the vessel got on their dignity, and we pointed to the rotten rigging to corroborate our opinions. The Navy Department ordered a court of inquiry, and all the ensigns were called before the court and individually questioned in regard to seamanship, their experience on the ocean, and their reasons for stating the rigging to be unfit for sea. It happened, for a wonder, that we six ensigns were all experienced seamen, and much above the average. The questions were promptly answered, and rather plainly, too. The court was composed of regular officers, and something must be done to exonerate the commandant at Boston. Volunteer officers were considered as interlopers, and tolerated only as a necessity. The result was that Acting-Master William D. Urann was deemed unfit to command a vessel, and was detached from the brig Perry and ordered to report for duty to the commandant of the Mississippi flotilla. He was there but a few weeks when his merits as an experienced officer were recognised, and he was promoted to acting lieutenant, ranking with a captain in the army.

I may as well explain the grades of rank now: A captain in the navy has rank with a colonel in the army; commander, with a lieutenant-colonel; lieutenant-commander, with a major; lieutenant, with captain; master, with first lieutenant; ensign, with second lieutenant.

The fact of our captain being relieved did not prevent orders being issued to have the brig repaired, and the riggers from the yard came on board and made things lively for a while.

In about a month's time we were ready, and started for Charleston. All went nicely until after we passed Cape Hatteras. I had an attack of some light fever, and was on the sick list. On board was a master's mate by the name of Bridges. He had been recommended for promotion to ensign, and ordered to Boston for examination, but, failing to pass, he was attached to the Perry, and every one on our vessel was desirous to assist him in gaining experience. For that reason he was allowed to stand my watch while I was sick, and usually some of the ensigns would be on deck to see that everything was all right. But early one evening we had just finished supper, and all of us sat in the ward-room having a social chat. Feeling as if some fresh-air exercise would benefit me, I went on deck, and, looking to the windward, I saw that a heavy squall would soon strike us. Mr. Bridges was serenely promenading the deck, totally oblivious of any impending danger, while the brig was sailing close to the wind with every stitch of canvas set. I told Bridges to have the light sails taken in as quickly as possible, at the same time calling his attention to the squall. No time was lost by me in getting to the ward-room, and informing the executive that he was needed on deck to have all hands shorten sail. While I was speaking, the squall struck us and nearly capsized the brig, and it was hard work for us to get on deck, on account of the vessel careening over so much. Then there was an exciting time; the crew had become panic-stricken for a few minutes. Orders were given to let go everything. The pressure of the wind, the mast lying at such a great angle, prevented the yards from coming down. The wheel was in front of the cabin door, the excitement brought the captain out, and he yelled to put the wheel hard down. Now that was the first time that he ever gave an order on deck, and it nearly ended the Perry's career, then and there.

The navigating officer has to stand regular deck watch with the others while at anchor, and the executive is expected to be on board during the day and have charge of everything in general. One of the master's mates—not Mr. Bridges—was also put on watch duty, and, with six ensigns, our turn on watch was only four hours out of every twenty-four; in fact, we had so much leisure time that we did not know how to pass it away. All the work required of the crew was to scrub decks before breakfast and a half-hour's drilling at the broadside guns. Arrants and myself would take a boat and crew and go fishing every pleasant day. Taking the sounding lead with us, we were soon able to find good fishing grounds. The bottom of the lead has a large hole that is filled with hard tallow—"arming the lead." When the lead strikes the bottom it will bring up anything that it comes in contact with, be it sand, mud, or gravel, and, if rocks, the tallow will bear the impression. By that means, it can be known to a certainty what the bottom is composed of in that locality. For fishing, we would sound until we found a bank composed of shells and gravel, and there we were sure of catching all the fish we wanted.

Now, for our captain's mistake No. 2. He had gotten the idea into his head that we were not close enough to the land. The weather had been quite pleasant and the sea smooth. An experienced seaman has no use for land unless it is in a secure harbour, and, much to our surprise, the captain ordered the sails loosened and the anchor weighed, and we stood in for the shore. The leadsman was continually taking soundings and, when in three fathoms, the brig was brought head to wind and the anchor let go. There we were in eighteen feet of water, the brig's draft being twelve feet. This left just six feet of water between our keel and a nice hard sandy bottom. The captain was well satisfied with the vessel's position, as he remarked that no blockade-runner could now pass without being seen. A few nights afterward his mind underwent a mighty sudden change, when a heavy gale came on from the eastward about midnight, and the waves got high and every few minutes the sea would lift us up, then let us down with a heavy thud on that "nice sandy bottom." The fact was we were anchored in the breakers. The top-sails were reefed and set, then the anchor was weighed, the foresail was braced sharp up and back, so as to bring the vessel's head to the southward, but it was of no use; the brig would not swing around in the breakers but only drift astern towards the beach. The anchor was again let go, then a rope was put into the hawse-hole, the other end outside the port and fastened on the quarter-deck. The cable was unshackled at the fifteen fathoms shackle, the rope fastened to it, and the chain let run out of the hawse-hole. As the brig drifted astern the rope fastened on the quarter gradually tautened until the strain on the anchor checked us, allowing the vessel to swing around until her top-sails filled. A buoy was then attached to the rope and the latter let go. Away we went, leaving the anchor behind, and then came the hard work in earnest——beating off a lee shore in a heavy gale of wind. When the gale was over we found our brig to the south-east of Charleston and a considerable distance from our station, so back we went as fast as the vessel would sail. While passing the entrance to Charleston Bay we espied a small schooner stranded on the shoals. Here was a chance to display our valour and zeal for the service.

Arrants and I were in charge of the second cutter, with the boat's crew heavily armed. When we got on the shoals we found the "suspicious" craft to be a small schooner of about fifteen tons. The sails were neatly furled and the cabin entrance carefully boarded up. There were neither cargo nor provisions on board, and on the stern, in freshly painted letters, was the name Old Abe, which we thought was strange for a rebel craft. There was not a house nor living being in sight in any direction, so we set fire to the mysterious craft and returned to the brig.

CHAPTER XIX
AFTER BLOCKADE-RUNNERS

ON arrival at Murrell Inlet, we sought the wooden buoy, and got it on board; the line was put through the hawse-pipe, and we all tugged at it until we got hold of the chain, when that was put around the windlass and the anchor hove up. Having had enough of that locality, we anchored farther out to sea in deeper water. In a couple of weeks, our nearest neighbour, the gun-boat at Georgetown Bay, brought us our mail and some fresh beef. They had a tale of woe to unfold. It seems they had captured a small schooner and made use of it as a pleasure yacht. One night it had broken adrift and stranded on some sand shoals. They had intended, some pleasant day, to fasten a rope to it and have the gun-boat pull it off, but they sorrowfully stated that the "—— rebs had burned it up." We hadn't a word to say. It was the Old Abe.

The enemy was in the habit of making night attacks on our vessels whenever they had the opportunity. It would have been an easy matter for them to send small boats and men from Charleston overland and make things quite lively for us. To prevent any surprise party coming on board, we put up the "boarding nettings" and kept men on guard in different parts of the brig. George Brinsmaid, one of the coloured men on board, was useless for going aloft, or anything else, for that matter, so he had extra guard duty to perform. He was given a loaded rifle and stationed at the port gangway. It made no difference how often the officer of the deck would go to him, that fellow was sure to be found asleep. I had bucketful after bucketful of water thrown on him during my watch, but it had no perceptible effect in keeping him awake, for he was constitutionally sleepy. The fact that he was so useless formed circumstances which resulted in his death.

I had become quite tired of doing nothing but fishing, so I asked the captain if I could take the "dingey," the smallest boat on a man-of-war, and with two men go into the Inlet on an exploring expedition. He was desirous to have me go and find out if any vessels were in there, and, selecting two volunteers from the crew, we were ready to leave the brig about daylight. The boat was landed close to the southern point at the entrance to the Inlet. I walked cautiously around the nearest house without finding any footprints in the soft, white sand. That convinced me that no one was in the house. Getting into the boat, I had the men row slowly into the Inlet, the high, dry, soft marsh grass concealing us from view of any one who might be in that locality. At the southern end of the Inlet we saw a schooner, which probably had run the blockade, and, as it was not prudent just then, we proceeded no farther in that direction; the northern branch was also explored, but nothing was to be found there. We had been absent from the brig nearly four hours; the captain had become uneasy on our account and had taken the first cutter with an armed crew to look for us. We met him at the entrance to the Inlet. When told of what we had seen, he concluded to go ashore himself on the northern point. There we managed to shoot a couple of razor-back hogs that had been feeding on the beach. We raised such a rumpus that the rebel cavalry were making preparations to give us a warm reception. Their camp was in the woods about a mile from the beach. We could see them saddling their horses and acting in an excited manner. We found out afterward that the rebels had only sixteen men in camp at that time. Having had all the fun and exercise we wanted on shore, and out of respect to the rebels, we got into the boats and returned to the brig.

A few nights afterward, we discovered a boat nearing the vessel. Hailing it, we were informed that some refugees wished to come on board. Consent being given, they came alongside, and, after asking a few questions, we allowed them to come on board. There were eight men in the party, all desirous of joining the Federal army. Their boat being old and leaky, we destroyed it. They gave us what information they could about the rebels. Two regiments of Georgia cavalry were guarding the coast, being divided into squads of sixteen to twenty men each, each squad a couple of miles distant from the other. The schooner had run the blockade some time previous, having brought in a general cargo of merchandise. As we were anxious to know all about the schooner, it was decided that Ensign Arrants and myself should take the first cutter, with the crew well armed, and land at daybreak on the beach. By walking across the land which separated the end of the Inlet from the beach, we would be safer than rowing the boat into the narrow Inlet. We landed without being seen by the rebels, and, getting on the schooner, we soon ascertained that preparations were being made to run the blockade with a cargo of turpentine. If we had only burned the old schooner there and then, it would have been a wise act on our part. As my instructions were not to destroy it, if there was any probability of its preparing for leaving the Inlet, I reluctantly ordered the men back to the boat and returned to the brig. A house was near the schooner in which was stored a large quantity of the turpentine, and some of the cavalry slept there, as we were informed by some of the refugees. By setting fire to everything we could have done considerable damage, besides capturing some prisoners. Captain Gregory was in favour of letting the schooner run out and then taking her as a prize, for turpentine was very valuable at that time and prize-money would make quite an addition to our pay.

About every week Arrants and myself would take a boat with six men and land on the southern point at the deserted house. By climbing I would get on the roof, and by the aid of powerful marine glasses I could see what progress was being made with loading on the schooner. Our last reconnoitring expedition nearly resulted in serious disaster. This time we had landed on the north point first. Arrants and I each had a rifle, but the six men forming the boat's crew were unarmed. While walking between the sand dunes, we espied a razor-back sow with two young pigs. I shot at the sow as she was running away. The bullet ploughed a deep gash in her back, which only increased her speed. We did not get her, but did capture the two little pigs alive. We were laughing and the porkers squealing, when I happened to look around and discovered a couple of mounted Confederates behind one of the sand dunes. They probably thought the boat's crew was armed, and for that reason did not attack it. However, we lost no time in getting into the boat with our pigs. The sand dunes are pyramids of sand from fifteen to twenty feet in height, and are caused by the strong winds drifting the dry, white sand on the beach. If those two men had had spunk enough, by keeping behind the dunes they could have made it very unpleasant for us in the boat, as the Inlet was not over fifty yards in width. We then landed on the southern point a distance from the house and, telling the crew to row slowly up the beach, pursued our investigations. We had reason to believe some one had been watching us, as there were fresh footprints in the sand leading from the deserted building to the one near the schooner, about half a mile distant.

When we got to the house I told Arrants that I would get on the house and take a look at the blockade-runner. The building stood on piles about six feet in height and, as the steps leading to the house were gone, it was necessary for me to do some climbing. I turned around to give my rifle to Arrants, and just then caught sight of about twenty cavalrymen coming from the other house towards us, and they seemed to be in a big hurry about it, too. We Yankees did not have any particular business to detain us there, so we made a hasty retreat for the boat. The latter was about fifty feet from the shore. I told the men to pull in quick. Arrants and myself ran into the water about knee deep. We caught the boat and stopped it from coming any farther. My companion and I then got into the craft in a very undignified style for officers. If the enemy had come right up to us they could have captured us without firing a shot, as we should have been perfectly helpless. Instead of doing so, they dismounted at the edge of the sand dunes and fired quite an assortment of lead at us from rifles, double-barrelled shotguns, and old-fashioned muskets carrying large bullets with three buckshot additional. They made us fellows feel nervous with their careless shooting. While the Southerners were shooting, we had to turn the boat completely around and head out to sea. The man with the bow oar tried to push the bow around by putting the blade of the oar on the hard sandy bottom and shoving it, and was so energetic that the oar snapped in two. At last we got around, and for a few minutes some good sprinting was done.

The coxswain in the stern then had the best chance of being struck by the bullets, and doubled himself in a way that would have aroused the envy of a contortionist. The men at the oars laid as low as possible for them to row. I was shoved out at full length, shoving at the stroke oar while the men pulled. Arrants was doing the same thing with the second oar. My left cheek was badly stung in different places—I supposed at first by buckshot—but a rifle ball had struck the handle of the oar on which I was shoving, and, my head being close to it, the splinters from the dry ash wood had struck in my face. That bullet had just barely missed my head. As soon as we got out of the range of the buckshot, Arrants and myself returned the fire with our rifles. The Confederates then quickly took their horses and got behind the sand dunes. The battle was over. One of our men had his right eyelid grazed by a buckshot just enough for a single drop of blood to ooze out. A rifle bullet went through the stern of the boat, passing between the coxswain's legs, thence between the whole boat's crew, until it reached the man in the bow, where it passed his left side and elbow, removing some cuticle from each. That fellow was scared, sure enough, at first, but after we pulled his shirt off to stop the blood and found the skin was only peeled off, he concluded to live a little while longer. It was a miracle that every one of us was not killed or seriously wounded. We were in a compact space and the enemy had nothing in the way of a counter-fire to prevent taking deliberate aim.

We got back to the brig, and handed up our prize pigs for Christmas gifts, then told of our adventure with the rebels. The boat was hoisted up and inspected. It had twenty-two buckshot marks, and was pierced through and through by six bullets. My face was badly spotted by the splinters from the oar. We were all congratulated upon our narrow escape. Captain Gregory vowed vengeance on the Southerners for their conduct, and, that night, plans were arranged for the next day to "carry the war into Africa." Then we went to bed, excepting those on duty.

Next morning at eight o'clock we tried again and sailed as close to the beach as possible and anchored. An officer was stationed aloft with a pair of marine glasses, that he might see over the sand dunes and have a good view of the rebel schooner. For three hours we tried to put a shell into the blockade-runner with our guns, but could not do so on account of the sand dunes interfering with our range. At twelve o'clock Captain Gregory decided to land a boat's crew; and that was his mistake No. 3. We all well knew there would be resistance offered to our landing, under the circumstances, but I received orders to set fire to the schooner, and therefore had nothing to say. Sixteen of the best men were selected and armed with rifles, and to each was also given a navy revolver, or else a boarding-pistol, carrying an ounce bullet. Arrants was ordered to assist me. The paymaster, a new officer from Boston, volunteered his services, for he thought he would have a picnic, and, besides, his admiring friends had presented him with an expensive sword and revolver, and these weapons he intended taking back home with him all covered with rebel gore. We three officers carried a whole arsenal—sword, rifle, and revolver. As we expected to meet not more than twenty Confederates, we felt confident of victory, especially as we were better armed and could load our guns more rapidly, having improved cartridges. The enemy had to tear the paper on theirs with their teeth, while ours could be used without that process, as they were encased in combustible paper.

CHAPTER XX
A PRISONER OF WAR

WE took the first cutter for a landing party, and the second cutter was manned with an armed crew of six men to take care of our boat while we were on shore. A small keg, filled with tarred rope yarns and a bottle of turpentine, was given to me with which to set the schooner on fire. I told Captain Gregory to send George Brinsmaid along with us to carry the keg, as he was of no use on the brig, and might be of some use on dry land. Everybody thought it would be a good joke, so Mr. Brinsmaid was ordered into the boat, and promoted to the office of bearer of combustibles. My instructions were plain enough: "To land and set fire to the schooner and house, and do all the damage possible."[D] In case we were attacked, we were to get behind the sand dunes and defend ourselves, while the guns on the brig would shell the rebels.

[D] It was denied afterward that any such order had been given.

All being ready, we started for the shore. Before landing, I had a long rope attached to the bow of our boat and fastened to the stern of the second cutter. When we got on shore, the second cutter towed our boat just clear of the surf, ready for us to get into in a hurry, with the bow headed towards the sea. George Brinsmaid had the keg to carry, and was placed in the centre of the party. Then we started for the sand dunes, intending to carry desolation and dismay into the Southern Confederacy.

When we got to the sand dunes, indications pointed strongly to the fact that we had got into a bad scrape. The sand was covered with a large number of horse tracks, as if a whole regiment of horses had been tramping around. I had not much time to take in the situation, as the enemy made a charge between us and the boats. They came in double file; the left file came for us, the right going for the boats. I looked at the brig, expecting to see the guns shelling the rebs on the open, but, much to my surprise, the captain had allowed the brig to swing around stern to shore, and not a gun could be brought to bear on the enemy.

I told the men to get behind the dunes and fire only at the enemy nearest to them. We were scattered a few feet apart so as not to be in a compact body. The first man came into view just in front of me. He was riding to the top of the dune. Knowing that the rifle would carry high at such a short distance, I aimed low at his breast. The bullet struck him square in the forehead and the horse gave a jump and threw him off, the body rolling down the steep dune to our feet. That checked the enemy for a few seconds, as they saw that it would be safer to attack us dismounted. For about five minutes that was a warm place. Buckshot, bullets, and sand were flying in all directions. The party attacking the boat were unsuccessful, so they circled around and got in our rear. Then we were completely surrounded and had to surrender. Two of the Confederates were killed and several wounded, and besides, they lost three horses. On our side two were killed, and nearly every one of us wounded. After we had surrendered, James Pinkham was lying face down on the ground, a bullet having passed through both of his hips, and, because he could not get up when ordered to do so, a rebel lieutenant shot him in the back with his revolver. A young Irishman by the name of Tobin, belonging to our party, had reloaded his rifle and was standing close to Pinkham. The rebel lieutenant said, "You — — Yankee, come here and give up your arms!" Tobin advanced with both hands stretched out, the rifle in his left and a boarding-pistol in his right. When he got within about fifteen feet of the lieutenant, he blazed away at him with the pistol, dropped it and ran across the salt marsh to the woods, about half a mile distant. He missed the lieutenant, but killed his horse. A cavalryman started after Tobin and, when near to him, called him to halt. Tobin turned around and pointed his rifle at the man. The latter's gun being empty, he halted, and off went the Irishman again for the woods. Another man started in pursuit with a loaded rifle, and, when close enough, he shot Tobin in the leg, and the poor fellow afterwards died in Andersonville Prison.

The Southerners who did not come until the fight was all over, did all the blustering and had the most to say. They did certainly call us anything but gentlemen, and also were very indignant because Brinsmaid had been taken prisoner. "You Yankee ——— ———, get in line there with your nigger brother!" was the first order we got. We were taken to the edge of the woods and everything was confiscated, whether of value or not. The enemy wrangled considerably among themselves, with the result that George Brinsmaid was taken to a tree about fifty yards from us, a horse's halter put around his neck, and he was hanged on one of the limbs; then two charges of buckshot were fired into his breast. The poor fellow never spoke a word after leaving the brig. In the fight his left hand had been shot off by buckshot, but not a groan was heard from him. Some of the Confederates proposed hanging all of us, on account of having a "nigger" with us, and, judging from what I had seen of their actions, I almost came to the conclusion that the proposition would be carried out. However, in a little while the excitement passed away and they began to be sociable. The wounded were all examined and wads of raw cotton put into the wounds. One man came to me with his left hand bandaged up. He inquired if I was badly hurt.

"Well," says he, "you're in luck to be alive now. I took deliberate aim at you as you stood with your back towards me while loading your rifle. My —— shotgun burst and blowed off three of my fingers, and that is what saved you."

In his eagerness to kill a Yankee, he had put too heavy a charge in his gun, and it had burst just where he gripped the barrels with his left hand. My sack coat was cut in several places. One shot struck me in the arm near the shoulder and went about six inches between the muscles towards the elbow. That little piece of lead has been my constant companion for just thirty-four years the 5th of December. I can always tell when wet weather is coming, by feeling a dull pain in my right arm. During the general conversation, I found out the cause of so many men being ready to receive us on shore. It seems that the first shell we had fired from the brig went very high over the schooner and landed in the camp in the woods. They were enjoying an after-breakfast smoke when it fell in their midst. It was laughable to hear them twitting each other about vacating their quarters. We could not make them believe that it was a chance shot. They insisted that one of the refugees on our vessel had pointed out their camp to us. They also believed that they had killed all the men but one in the boat the day before. Arrants and myself told them that we were the two officers on shore, but they would have it that we were both killed. The continual report of our broadside guns had been heard for quite a distance north and south of Murrell Inlet. All the rebel pickets thought that a blockade-runner had been run ashore by the Yankees, so all hastened to the scene of action, especially as there might be a prospect of looting the vessel if ashore. When they arrived and found out the true state of affairs they concluded to remain, in the hope that we would send men ashore to burn the schooner. There were present two companies of cavalry—one each from the Fifth and Twenty-first Georgia Regiments and under command of Captains Bowers and Harrison. There was where Captain Gregory made a blunder in sending us ashore after cannonading the schooner. Instead of a few men to contend with, we had a force of one hundred and twenty to give us a warm reception, which they did in most orthodox style.

If still living, one of those misguided men is telling his grandchildren how he captured my sword, for which I had paid twenty-five good dollars. The rifle and the revolver belonged to the Government.

At four o'clock that afternoon we started for Charleston, S. C. Those who were too badly wounded to walk were put in an old wagon. Our boat's coxswain had been hit in the head with a number of buckshot. He must have had a tough skull, as the shot cut furrows in his scalp and removed some of his hair. The blood flowed very freely. He was compelled to walk the whole distance. We had a guard of ten men, under command of the lieutenant that Tobin had tried to kill. Well, that fellow made things as unpleasant as possible for us, in order to have revenge for the killing of his horse. The road was composed of white, dry sand, and at every step we took we would sink to our ankles. The cavalry horses were fast walkers, and we had to keep up with them. We came to a stream of cold water, and we were forced to wade through it. There was a footbridge for pedestrians on one side of the road, but we were not allowed to go over it. The cavalrymen got on their knees on the saddles, and their horses, plunging through the water, splashed it over our heads; consequently, we got a good drenching. Walking was more difficult for us weighted with water; besides, it was night-time, and in the month of December—rather late in the season for a cold-water bath.

At nine o'clock in the evening we arrived at our destination, Georgetown Bay, having walked, or rather been driven, twenty-five miles in five hours' time. It was all we could do to keep up with the horses. A squad was in our rear with orders to run us down if we lagged behind. We were placed in an old log house, the floor being covered to the depth of two inches with sheep-manure. The wounded were laid in the filth, without anything being done towards making them comfortable. Two pailfuls of small, raw sweet potatoes were given us for our supper. That night, December 5, 1863, will never be erased from my memory; tired and sore in every limb, my feet badly swollen, the wounded arm hurting, wet and hungry, I lay down in the manure and tried to sleep, but could not; the cold and the wet clothes kept me chilled through and through. The poor fellows who were wounded were continually moaning, but we were powerless to alleviate their misery.

We had plenty of reason for growling about the quality of our potato supper, but the following morning's breakfast was omitted altogether. About nine o'clock we were divided into squads and taken across the bay in sailboats. Those who were badly wounded were taken to the hospital; the rest of us were placed in the Georgetown jail, and a dirty room about twelve feet square was kindly placed at our disposal. At three in the afternoon we had breakfast, dinner, and supper combined. The menu consisted only of one dish—a pan of cold boiled rice. With a piece of stick it was cut into equal shares, and each man took his portion in his hand and devoured it at his leisure. We remained there five days. The only event of interest which occurred there was my being taken out to General Tropier's headquarters. He asked a few questions about the gunboat which was blockading the entrance to Georgetown Bay. My answers were rather evasive. Then I did some talking about the treatment we had received after being taken prisoners. He said that in future we would not be abused while under his control.

About four o'clock of the fifth day we were taken from the jail, and, with a cavalry guard, we were started for Charleston, S. C. It was a triangular journey. Straight down the coast Charleston was distant sixty miles, but the Yankees had the water routes, and consequently we had to walk forty-three miles west to King's Tree, the nearest railroad station. Thence, by railroad, we were taken sixty-five miles southeast to Charleston. Lieutenant Burroughs was in charge of the party. He allowed us to walk at an ordinary gait, and was very kind and civil to us.

CHAPTER XXI
IN THE PRISON

AT nine o'clock we arrived at the Black River Ferry, where a halt was made for the night. We were then taken into the ferryman's house. Lieutenant Burroughs ordered supper for four. Arrants, the paymaster, and myself were invited by him to supper. It was the only time I had a civilized meal while in the Confederacy. We all slept on the hard floor, a fire in the room keeping us warm. At daylight we crossed the river on a primitive ferry. A rope was fastened to each bank of the river, and an old-flat boat was held in place by it, and pulled back and forth by hand power. At noon we halted for a rest and to cook the dinner—some more boiled rice. Late at night we arrived at King's Tree. The next day, in the afternoon, we got to Charleston, and were at once given in charge of the provost-marshal. After the taking of our names and rank the party was separated. The sailors were escorted to the jail by a guard, and a young lieutenant very politely informed us that we would go with him by a different route, so as not to attract the attention of the citizens. He took us through the burnt district.

What a wonderful change there was since I had last been in that city! All business was suspended. A large area was in ruins from the fire, grass was growing in the streets, and there was desolation everywhere. We could plainly hear the guns firing from our batteries on Norris Island. On arriving at the jail, the lieutenant shook hands with us and bade us good-bye. We were taken to the top floor and had an entire corridor to ourselves. There being about sixteen large cells, twelve feet square, we had plenty of room— in fact, each of us could have had an entire suite to himself had he desired it.

Everything looked very familiar to me, as it was the same place in which I was confined before my trial in 1856. The newspapers, giving an account of our capture, stated that I was supposed to be the same George Thompson who had been tried in the United States District Court for murder a few years previously. On account of the notice in the newspapers in regard to my being a prisoner of war and confined in the jail, a number of citizens visited me, but, having no permit from the commandant, they had their trouble for nothing. Major John Ryan, chief of subsistence on General Beauregard's staff, and an old friend of my father, was the only person allowed to see me. Our interview was quite sociable at first, then we gradually became belligerent, while conversing about the war and its issues. He had questioned me about my rank and the amount of pay I received in the Federal navy. Then the proposition was made that I join the rebel navy with the rank of lieutenant. When I refused, he became exceedingly wrathy. Finally he cooled down a little, and said that General Beauregard would send for me very soon, as he wished to have an interview with me. I replied that it would only be waste of time for him to do so. Now, from the questions that had been asked me, I knew exactly what the rebs wanted to know. They had sent out a torpedo boat to sink the Ironsides, but it was a failure. An ensign was killed by a rifle-bullet from the torpedo boat, but no damage was done to the ship when the torpedo exploded. Admiral Dahlgren had ordered a raft of timber to be placed all around the Ironsides in order to prevent any more torpedo boats getting near enough to do any damage. The rebs could see with telescopes from Sumter that the Yankee sailors were hard at work around the ship, but could not find out what was being done. The Charleston papers stated that the Ironsides was in a sinking condition, and could only be kept above water by the use of heavy timbers. That same torpedo boat afterward destroyed the Housatonic, but the boat and crew were never seen afterward. In all probability they blew themselves up at the same time.

General Beauregard retained all officers captured by his troops in case he should need them as hostages. Consequently, Columbia, S. C, was to be our place of abode, instead of Libby Prison at Richmond, where the officers were generally confined. While in the Charleston jail we heard from our friends quite frequently. Gilmore's guns would send shells into the city. They sounded like a heavy wagon-wheel going over a rough pavement. Next would be a heavy thud, and, in a few seconds more, a terrible explosion. At first, percussion shells were used, but quite a large percentage of them would turn in their flight through the air, and as they would not strike fuse first, no explosion would take place. A lot of men were always watching for such shells to strike. With shovels and pickaxes they would dig them out of the ground. The rebel ordnance department paid one hundred dollars in Confederate currency for every unexploded shell delivered. The next move was for the Yankees to change from percussion to time fuses. The first shell did not explode on striking, so a crowd, as usual, started to unearth it. Quite a number of spectators were watching the fun. Suddenly the operations were suspended. The time fuse exploded the shell, killing several persons and wounding a number more. Of course the Yankees were loudly cursed for playing such a mean trick, but the ordnance department got no more of our shells. The second day after our arrival a shell passed over the jail and landed in a frame building only a block distant. When it exploded, timbers and boards flew in all directions. We could see the dust and splinters in the air quite plainly from our window. Somehow, I felt pleased whenever one of those missiles came along, although we were liable to be killed at any time by one of them.

Much to my surprise, a single mattress and blanket were sent up to me by some of my former acquaintances. I considered it only proper that such good fortune should be shared with Arrants and the paymaster, so we used the mattress for a pillow, and, by sleeping "spoon fashion," we made the blanket cover us all. I may state now that it was the only time that we had a blanket during our entire imprisonment. In all of that part of the building there was no furniture of any description. We had to utilize the floor for all purposes. Our food consisted of cold boiled rice, and was brought to us twice a day in a tin pan. Table etiquette was dispensed with for the time being, and our fingers had to be used for disposing of the food. The evening of the seventh day some of the provost guard took us to the railroad depot en route for Columbia. While waiting for the train to start, a couple of women got into conversation with us. They bade us "Good luck" and handed us each a quart bottle of corn whisky. The provost guard drank the most of it. At any rate, it helped to pass away the night in a cheerful manner. In the morning we arrived at the Richland County jail, Columbia, S. C. That was to be our resting-place for several months.

The following is the substance of the official report of our capture, etc., made to the Secretary of the Navy by Admiral Dahlgren:

"Two boys who had been sent on shore in the dingey at Murrell Inlet for a barrel of sand for holystoning decks had been killed by the rebels. A few weeks later Acting Ensign Myron W. Tillson, with thirteen men, were captured at the same place while trying to burn a blockade-runner. Believing Acting Master Gregory to be a discreet and experienced officer, I sent his vessel to blockade the Inlet, also instructing him not to send any men on shore. Three officers and sixteen men were also captured from his vessel. I inclose his report. On a personal interview he claimed that his orders were not obeyed by Acting Ensign Arrants, and that the latter was responsible for the capture of the men. Having had so much trouble at Murrell Inlet, I decided to send a strong force of marines and sailors to that place to destroy the schooner and other property, as well as to remove any disposition to exult on the part of the rebels for capturing so many of our men."

Then followed the report of the expedition as made by Acting Master Gregory, detailing the amount of damage done. The Secretary of the Navy then issued the following general order, which was read at general muster on each vessel in the squadron:

"GENERAL ORDERS, NO. ——.

"For flagrant disobedience of orders from his commanding officer and being responsible for a number of men having been captured by the rebels, Acting Ensign William B. Arrants is dismissed from the United States

Navy. While the Department does not wish to discourage acts of gallantry or enterprise, strict obedience of orders must be insisted on.

"GIDEON WELLES,

"*Secretary of the Navy.*"

The whole blame had been put upon Arrants. Upon my arrival in Washington, I reported to the Secretary of the Navy in person, giving him a full report of the whole affair in writing. He asked me a number of questions in regard to Captain Gregory. As the naval records showed that my commission antedated that of Arrants by about three months, it proved conclusively that Captain Gregory had misrepresented when he stated that the expedition had been commanded by Arrants. A great injustice had been done. An order was at once issued restoring Acting Ensign William B. Arrants to the naval service from the date of dismissal.

Captain Gregory, in order to screen himself, had put all the blame on Arrants, supposing him to be dead. When he found out we were about to be exchanged he concluded that it was about time for him to resign from the service. By that means he escaped from serious consequences which would have resulted from his conduct. The punishment meted out by court-martial was generally severe during the time of the Rebellion.

CHAPTER XXII
PRISON LIFE AND PRISON FARE

ELEVEN naval officers gave us a most cordial reception when the captain in charge of the prison introduced us as fresh fish. All were eager to learn the latest news of the war, and especially about the prospects of exchanging prisoners of war in the near future. Now it happened that we were well posted on the "exchange" question—namely, that the authorities at Washington had notified the rebels that the cartel was ended, and no more exchanges would be made. Our men, when received, were disabled from duty on account of sickness caused by lack of proper food and clothing, as well as inhuman treatment. On the other hand, the rebels were returned in better health and more comfortably clothed than at the time of capture. The advantage to the rebel army, under the circumstances, would be too great to permit of any further exchanges. It was policy to let the Union men remain as prisoners, as they would be useless for a long time for active duty. Keeping the rebels in prison would deprive the rebel army of a large number of able men, who, released, would be immediately available for active duty.

Our fellow-prisoners were down-hearted at first, when told the dictum; but soon their cheerful remarks showed that they believed our Government was pursuing a wise course under the circumstances. The jail was a three-story building, the two lower floors being used exclusively for the confinement of debtors. The third story was fitted up with cells for the criminals. At that time there was no State prison in South Carolina. The longest sentence a prisoner could receive was two and one half years in jail. Murder, robbery, burglary, arson, and rape were punishable by death. A man whose punishment was commuted from death could only be confined for the maximum jail sentence. We fourteen naval officers were confined in one room on the first floor. The size of the apartment was sixteen by twenty feet. When we lay on the floor at night there was but little vacant space. Sixteen army officers were confined in a room on the other side of the main hall. One half-hour in the morning and in the afternoon was allowed us to go into the yard, in order to wash and attend to our toilet, and only four were permitted to go at one time. For that reason we had to be in a hurry, so as to give all an opportunity. When the half-hour had expired, we were counted and the door locked. The army officers were then let out for the same length of time. We received our rations every ten days, in an uncooked condition. Unbolted corn-meal was the staple food. Two ounces of old, mouldy bacon was allowed each person for the ten days, that being the only animal food we received. Sometimes a small quantity of rice was also allowed. In the yard was a small brick building used as a kitchen, where the cooking was done. Opposite, and extending the whole length of the yard, was an old wooden barracks in which were confined about sixty privates. One private was detailed for the navy and one for the army officers. Not much skill was required for the cooking, but considerable ingenuity was needed to devise ways and means. In our mess the officers had managed to get a table, two long benches, ten pie-plates, and some knives and forks. Two meals a day was all that our rations would stand. This was our regular menu for about nine months for every meal: Corn-meal, slapjacks, corn-bread, corn-meal gravy, and corn-meal coffee. Our bacon was used for making the gravy and greasing the old tin pan which we utilized as a griddle. Corn-meal was burned nearly black for making the coffee. At one time our rations missed connections for nearly two days, and there was woe and agony. We divided the time about equally in damning the Confederacy and praying for something to eat. There were two iron-barred windows in our room which overlooked the yard of our next-door neighbour. A man, wife, and little boy lived there. A passage way about twelve feet wide separated the jail and a one-story cottage. One of our windows was exactly opposite their bedroom window, but both too high from the ground for the rebel sentry on guard in the passage way to see into either of them. Our neighbour's name was Crane. The family were strong Unionists, and we carried on a daily conversation by slate-writing. All the latest news was given to us, as well as any information which we desired.

Mr. Crane was a young man about thirty years of age, and he had a special permit from the rebel government exempting him from military service, on account of being a wagon-maker and needed by the citizens in Columbia to do their work. A girl about eighteen years old finally came to reside with the family. We immediately christened her "Union Mary," and kept that girl busy receiving and throwing kisses at us. She seemed to have nothing else to do but to watch our window. As we had plenty of leisure time, some one of the party was continually making distant love to her. At last she let us know that she wanted to go North and live with the Yankees. Nearly all of us wrote a letter telling her how to get a pass through the lines and recommending her to our relatives. She succeeded all right. The father of one of the officers got her a good situation and gave her a fine start in life, out of gratitude for the news which she brought him from his son.

A few weeks afterward Mr. Crane was ordered to report for military duty at Richmond. He and several companions got off the cars at the nearest point to our lines and were successful in getting through. The next we heard of him was through his wife, who said that he had reached New York city and was earning very high wages at his trade.

A company of home guards, composed of fifty men under command of a captain, first, second, and third lieutenants, were our guardian angels. The guard-room adjoined ours on the first floor. Their camp was outside the city limits. Every morning, at eight o'clock, the relief would come in and remain on duty for twenty-four hours. We became well acquainted with all, and were quite sociable. Three of the privates let us know that they were Union sympathizers. Many a favour they did for us, by assisting us to communicate with Union people in the city. In the month of March, 1864, all hopes of being exchanged before the ending of the war were given up. Every one of us was in favour of making an attempt to escape from prison, if possible. Lieutenant Preston and myself were to do the engineering part; the others agreed to work under our instructions. Preston was a regular officer, and myself being a volunteer removed any cause for believing that any favouritism would be shown during the progress of building a tunnel. After eight in the evening the guards never opened our door. Then we commenced operations.

A large brick fire-place was situated between the two windows. The bricks on one end were taken up and a hole was made that allowed us to get under the floor. Preston and myself worked nearly all night. First, we stopped up several ventilating holes with pieces of clay and brick. All the brickbats were piled in a corner to be out of our way. We found there would be plenty of space to pile up the dirt that would be taken from the tunnel, the height of the floor from the ground being about three feet. Directly under the window facing Crane's house we started a shaft three feet square. The dirt, as we removed it, was piled over the ventilating hole; there being no danger of any noise being heard by the sentry in the alley or a light seen, we ceased operations for the night. The bricks in the fire-place were replaced, and we retired for the night to our luxurious couches—the bare floor—for much-needed rest. The entrance to our lower regions must be attended to first, as the bricks had a very insecure foundation. One of the guards very kindly consented to carry our compliments and a request to Mrs. Crane for the loan of a saw, hammer, nails, and a piece of board, as we wished to make a shelf. During the afternoon we had everything in readiness. The bricks were removed and put in a soap box, cleats were hastily nailed to the floor timbers, pieces of board laid across, and the bricks replaced. Ashes were then filled into the cracks. It was a first-class job when finished, and we could defy detection. One of us went into the kitchen in the yard and stole our own poker from the cook. It was a piece of flat iron, and the only instrument procurable for excavating purposes. The officers were divided into working parties, two in each squad, each to work two hours at a time.

Preston would direct and assist in the work, from eight until twelve midnight, and I from twelve to four in the morning.

It was necessary to be careful about the construction of the tunnel, as it was to be run under a sentry's feet. If there should happen to be a cave-in and a reb drop down among the toilers, it would be rather embarrassing. Crane's house was built in the Southern style for all wooden buildings, resting on supports about two feet in height. Our objective point was about the centre of his habitation. We could crawl to the other side, and by getting over a board fence would practically become "prisoners-at-large."

The ground was favourable for our work, being composed of stiff red clay. All felt happy and cheerful as the work progressed, and the monotony of being so closely confined was somewhat relieved. On the corner of the square in which the jail was located was the city hall. We could hear the hours and half hours as they were struck, quite plainly, so we had no trouble about the time of quitting work. It was necessary for us to have a point to start our measurements from, and after much discussion, we selected a window-sill in our room directly over the tunnel-shaft. It was a strange place to locate it, but from that point every part of the work was measured to an inch. By fastening a wad of wet paper to a thread we ascertained the exact distance between Crane's house and the inside of the jail wall. One of us held the thread on the window-sill while the other kept throwing the wad until it struck the clapboard. When the sentry walked past our window he gave us the opportunity, and, by lowering the wad to the ground, we got the height of the passage-way which the sentry patroled. The shaft was sunk nine feet, and was considerably lower than the foundation of the building. Then the tunnel was started, being two feet wide and three feet in height, the top being arched. For a distance of fourteen feet it was perfectly level, then it was started on an angle towards the surface of the ground.

About that time we had to stop operations for a few days. Orders had been sent by General Beauregard to put Lieutenant-Commander E. P. Williams and Ensign Benjamin Porter in irons, and hold them as hostages for a rebel naval lieutenant, who was sentenced to be hanged by the Federal Government for piracy on Lake Erie. Williams was selected as the highest in rank, Porter for the reason that he had the most influential friends. The two officers were shackled together, hands and legs, and were doomed to be inseparable companions for the time being, with a chance of being hanged. Not knowing but that the officers or guards might enter our room during the night to look at the hostages, it was deemed advisable to leave the tunnel alone. The handcuffs and shackles were of the old style, shutting together by a spring bolt. To open them the key was inserted, and turning it a number of times would screw the bolt back. The key and spindle had threads cut like a common bolt and nut. Sailors understood the mechanism perfectly. By taking a piece of soft wood the size of the keyhole and boring a hole in the centre slightly smaller than the spindle, and twisting it around in the keyhole, threads would be cut in it, and the handcuffs opened. Another plan was to make a slip-noose of fine twine, and by slipping it over the spindle, the bolt could also be drawn back. During business hours our two unfortunate companions were fettered together, but the remainder of the time they could meander around separately. We had plenty of amusement in drilling them to get into proper position for being shackled as soon as there was any indication of the door being opened.

Supplementary orders soon arrived that Porter and Williams should be confined by themselves in a separate room. A small room next to that of the army officers was selected. Being on the first floor, it was an easy matter for us to release them when we were ready to escape. Work was at once resumed. Our greatest difficulty was in getting candles enough to supply us with light. Finally, the last night's work was finished. The tunnel was twenty-two feet in length. According to our diagram we were six inches from the surface of the ground under Crane's house. We were afraid to make a small hole to the surface to make sure that our measurements were correct, for if there should be any depression in the ground, the first rainstorm would let the water into our excavation. We divided ourselves into parties of two or three, each to select our own route to the Federal lines. A small school atlas was borrowed, and maps made of the different routes we intended to take. Lieutenant Brower, Arrants, and myself decided to go south twenty-five miles, and follow the Santee River east to the sea-coast, then taking our chances of reaching a Federal gunboat. Corn-meal was baked brown, and with a little salt added, by mixing it with water it would be ready for eating. Matches were put into bottles to prevent them from getting wet. In fact, all preparations were made for our journey that we could think of.

It occasionally happens that people make fools of themselves in assisting others. Well, that is just what we did; some of us thought it would not be right to leave the army officers behind. A vote was taken and all were in favour of giving the army officers a chance to go with us. They were notified and one week's time given them in which to get ready. They were instructed to be cautious, and that we would make an opening in their fire-place also as soon as Porter and Williams were released. The latter were to have the first chance for their liberty.

CHAPTER XXIII
DISAPPOINTMENT AND MORE WAITING

ABOUT the second day afterward circumstances indicated that our intention to escape was known to the officers of the guard. They would come into our room, ostensibly for a friendly visit, but we noticed that they were examining the windows and floor while chatting with us. Within a foot of the building was a six-foot board fence, and that was taken away, giving the sentry on duty a full view of our side of the walls. Then we knew, for certain, that something was wrong. On Saturday morning permission was obtained to have the room floor scrubbed. Everything was piled on the table and a general housecleaning took place. All of us then went into the yard until the floor got dry. As we anticipated, the officer on duty went into the room during our absence and gave it a thorough inspection, but nothing was discovered. We congratulated ourselves upon the successful issue of our game of bluff.

Sunday night, about eight o'clock, we heard an unusual noise in the guard-room, which sounded very much like sawing a hole in the floor. After a while the racket ceased, and we resumed our slumbers. Suddenly our room door was opened, Captain Sennes with several of the guards walked in, some armed with muskets and others with lighted candles. We were counted and reported as "all present."

"Gentlemen, I have found your hole!" was the startling announcement.

The whole affair was so ludicrous and unexpected that we began laughing. Captain Sennes was excited, and well pleased with the idea of having discovered our plan of escape.

"Now, gentlemen, I shall have to keep a guard in your room for the remainder of the night."

Of course we had no objections. About three o'clock in the morning he changed his mind and ordered us to be escorted into the room occupied by Williams and Porter. All the little portable articles we possessed, which might tempt the cupidity of the rebs, were hastily gathered up and our change of quarters soon effected. There was no more sleep for us. So much excitement in one night was too much for our delicate systems.

In the morning Captain Sennes concluded to confine the navy and army officers on the second floor. That part of the building was the "bull pen" for the conscripts. Every part of South Carolina was thoroughly searched for shirkers from military duty. The "poor whites," as they were called, would be taken from their families, manacled two together, and brought to the jail. When a squad of fifty was obtained, they would be sent to the front and distributed among different regiments. As a class they were very ignorant, but few of them knowing what the war was about.

"What do you 'uns want to come down here and whip we 'uns for?" was their only argument. But at the same time they would fight—there was no mistaking that fact.

Our new quarters were very uncomfortable in many respects: there were dirt and filth everywhere. An old box-stove in a small room was our fire-place. The conscripts had no firewood, so they had used the doors and frames for fuel, then the window-sashes and casings were utilized, and next was the lath from the partitions. That floor had plenty of ventilation. No difference which way the wind would come from, we got the full benefit of it. The rooms were divided between us, the army taking one side of the building, the naval officers the other, the hall-way being used as a promenade by all the tenants. No attempt was made to keep us separate as in the past, for the reason that the doors and partitions were lacking. The view of the city in our locality was very good. When we got tired of looking from one side of the building we could cross over and take a view in the opposite direction. The newspapers had blood-curdling articles in regard to our attempt at escaping. We were alluded to as "Yankee hirelings," and other pet names were bestowed upon us. Even poor Mrs. Crane got a roasting because her house happened to be over the exit of the tunnel. Quite a number of visitors came to the jail to view our work, but finally the whole affair became stale and forgotten. Then it occurred to Captain Sennes that it would be quite proper to plug the hole up. He was very anxious to know who engineered the work, but, very naturally, every one was bashful about claiming that honour. At last he unbosomed himself: "Gentlemen, as you constructed the tunnel, probably you can inform me how to fill it up." Now that question was a poser to all of us. A great many suggestions were made, but all proved unsatisfactory. Finally, the captain had the shaft filled up with brickbats and broken bottles. In the passage-way between the two buildings they dug down to the tunnel and put in a load of clay. With every rainstorm the clay would settle and leave a big hole. From observation and much debating on the subject, it was conceded that the proper plan would have been to dig it up from end to end. Our new quarters were quite uncomfortable. I devised all sorts of schemes to keep myself warm at night. Sleeping on a bare floor, the lack of blankets, and the cold wind, made a combination which it was useless to contend against. All I could do was to wait patiently for daylight, and then, by walking and exercising, get myself warmed up.

The sixty privates in the yard also caught the tunnel mania. The barracks had a wooden floor. Two boards were removed, and an excavation made to the rear of the building. The exit was in an adjoining garden. Not much skill in engineering was displayed on their part. They simply dug until they felt like stopping. The distance from the surface was ascertained by pushing a stick up through the ground. It was left there projecting above the surface. We were informed of their plans and intention to escape that night. It seems that Captain Sennes was also fully posted as to what was going on. A number of the rebs were stationed in the garden. The stick projecting from the ground indicated the place from which the prisoners would emerge. Orders were given to let a number of the Yankees come out, then to fire into the crowd and kill as many as possible. Fortunately, the first man to come out—Peter Keefe—happened to see one of the rebs. He gave the alarm to his companions. Being still on his hands and knees, he thought his best chance would be in making a bold run for liberty. As he jumped up a reb fired, the bullet shattering Keefe's left knee. The leg had to be amputated. The next day all the privates were removed from the yard and confined with us. That made affairs still worse, there being hardly space enough for us to lie down at night. Two escaped prisoners from Andersonville were added to our numbers. They arrived late at night, and, as it was dark, we could not see what they looked like. The lieutenant of the guard asked us to find a place for them to lie down. Brayton slept on the table. Calling the men, he said they could find room enough underneath.

After daylight we gathered around our new companions. They were still handcuffed together. It was a pitiful sight to look at them, dirty and ragged, with their ankles swollen up by scurvy. The face of one of them was badly swollen, and covered with pustules. The surgeon was at once sent for. He pronounced it to be small-pox. The sick man was sent to the pest-house; his companion was isolated in the barracks. The first one finally recovered, but his companion caught the infection and died. In a few days Brayton showed symptoms of small-pox, was removed to the pest-house, and also died. William Brayton was a sail-maker in the United States navy; his rank was that of warrant officer, a distinct grade from the line or staff officers. He was wounded and taken prisoner during the midnight surprise attack on Fort Sumter by the navy. A bullet had shattered his right forearm, and also went through the fleshy part of his right leg. Fortunately Captain Sennes realized the danger of having the officers and privates confined together. Besides, it was not a customary thing on either side, and, consequently, the privates were returned to the barracks in the yard, much to our satisfaction. They had the freedom of the yard nearly all day, which made them satisfied with the change.

I commenced to feel sick and discouraged, and had an inclination to lie on the floor continually. The surgeon examined me and gave me some quinine pills, saying that I probably had malarial fever. For several mornings he visited me, and was very particular about looking at my tongue. Finally a peculiar white mark showed on the tip end. There was no mistaking that mark. I had typhoid fever. Orders were given to send for the ambulance, and have me taken to the hospital. A large church on the outskirts of the town was to be my future abode. It was called the Second North Carolina Hospital. Why it received that name I could never find out. Opposite to it was the beautiful mansion and grounds belonging to General Wade Hampton, the pride of South Carolina. That misguided hero went through the war all right, only to lose a leg afterward, most unromantically, by a kick from a mule.

CHAPTER XXIV
A CRACKER BEAUTY

A PAROLE was made out for me to sign, but it was very difficult for me to sign my name. I managed to keep on my feet for a few hours, and the change and novelty seemed to give me strength. Early in the evening I undressed and got into bed, and there I remained for six weeks. Surgeon Thompson told me I had the "slow" typhoid fever, that I would have to be very patient, and not to worry. Most of the time I was in a stupor, but had a dim consciousness of what was passing around me. One of the privates from the yard had the fever. He arrived a few days after myself. Milk punch was given to him; within a week he died. My treatment was different. The medicine tasted like turpentine and camphor. But no milk punch was given me at any time. At last the fever broke and I slowly recovered. Large bed-sores made their appearance on both hips. In fact I was sore all over from lying in bed such a long time. At a distance of twenty-five feet every object would quadruple to my vision. If there was one man, I would see four. Any object hanging on the wall especially strengthened the optical delusion.

When able to sit up on my bed I would talk to Peter Keefe. His cot was just across the passage-way from my own. The amputation was skilfully done, but it took a long time for the stump to heal up. He did not care so much for the loss of the leg as he did for the failure of the plan to escape.

Two "Cracker" girls swept the basement floor and brought us our food. They may have been styled nurses on the pay-rolls for all I know. However, I made a great mistake in not making love to both, comparing them to angels, and trying to make them believe that they had saved me from an early grave. Instead I would make critical remarks about their lack of charms to Keefe, in their presence. The younger one was about twenty years of age. She wore low calfskin shoes and white stockings which needed a good washing. Many of my remarks referred to their soiled condition. While manipulating the broom she displayed wonderful talent for going to sleep. About every tenth movement she would stand still, resting on the broom-handle, and take a short nap. Then would follow another few strokes and more nap, the same routine continuing until the job was finished.

The hospital steward was also of the "Cracker" type, and a most devout Methodist. Somehow we were not bosom friends. He was very much afraid I would say something to shock the "sweeping beauty." Finally I got tired of his infernal canting and tersely told him to go to the devil, advising him at the same time to marry the girl with the dirty stockings, as I was very certain he was the right man for the husband. Events were quiet for a couple of days. Hostilities soon broke out. The doctor had ordered a soft-boiled egg to be given me. Beauty brought it to me in a glass tumbler and skipped away in a hurry. There was more salt than egg. Fortunately, she had not stirred it up, so I skimmed off the egg carefully and ate it. Then I gazed at the tumbler. There was at least one inch of solid salt in the bottom. Keefe had been watching me and was highly amused. But Beauty discreetly kept out of my way for the remainder of the day. I informed the surgeon that I was very dainty about eating eggs and preferred them served in the shell; so that salt racket was stopped. I will always believe that Beauty and her acting husband put up a job on me.

A very angular woman with sanctimonious visage and a huge Bible in her hand squatted herself by my bed. The way she read the Scriptures to me would make a dead man turn over in his coffin. In about five minutes there was war in earnest. The surgeon happened to come in just then and ordered her out of the hospital. The next episode was through a friendly German. He was a sailor, and, being in one of the Southern ports during the early of the Rebellion, he, like many other sailors, was forced into the rebel army. In one of the battles he had been wounded by a piece of shell. As he was now convalescent, he was at leisure to go where he pleased. He spoke about the large quantities of blackberries that were to be found in the woods. I asked him to bring me some the next time he gathered any. While taking a morning nap a plate of nice, large blackberries had been left on the table at my bedside. When I awoke I was perfectly delighted at the sight. I had been craving for fruit for some days past. They seemed too nice to eat. Temptation was strong, however, and I picked up a single berry and put it in my mouth. My intention was to eat the whole plateful—one at a time. The surgeon just then passed near me.

"Well, surgeon, this is a great treat," I said to him. He seemed quite nervous when he saw the berries.

"How many have you eaten?"

"This is the first one," I replied.

"Well, that is lucky for you. Had you eaten twelve of them, you would have been a dead man inside of twenty-four hours." He asked who gave them to me. Well, that I knew nothing about, as I was asleep and supposed that Beauty had left them for me. He took away the plate and went after Beauty. My German sailor friend was not found out, but the chasm between Dirty Stockings and myself was greatly widened.

I soon became convalescent. A reb with a loaded musket escorted me back to my old quarters in the jail. My fellow-prisoners gave me a cordial reception. It was at one time thought by them that I would remain permanently in the South. All monotony in our prison life was now over. Exciting news was heard every day. Sherman's army was marching through Georgia. The rebs were drawing our troops away from their base of supplies. All the "invading hirelings" were to be killed, gobbled up, and other dire calamities were to befall them. Wheeler's cavalry went howling through Columbia on their way to annihilate Sherman's "bummers." The citizens cheered, and the ladies waved their handkerchiefs and threw kisses at them. Those fellows were going to raise ——— sure enough. We had a good view of the whole proceeding from our window. A few cat-calls were given by us to help along the excitement. Not many weeks afterward that same cavalry went through Columbia again, but their noses were pointed in the opposite direction, with Sherman's cavalry not many miles in the rear. Those gallant defenders of the South looted all the stores on Main Street, and carried all they could conveniently get away with. No ladies threw kisses at them that time.

The Yankee officers confined in Libby Prison were removed to Charleston and placed under the fire of the Federal guns in hopes that the shelling of the city would be stopped. Through some means, the locality in which the prisoners were confined was made known to the Union troops, consequently none were killed. Several changes of localities were made, always with the same result. Finally the rebel provost-marshal and several of his guards were killed by Yankee shells, and then the prisoners were all sent to Columbia and confined in a stockade on the other side of the river—"Camp Sorghum," as it was christened by the Yankees. The prisoners at Andersonville were hastily sent to different parts of the Confederacy to keep them out of reach of Sherman's troops.

"Gentlemen, there will arrive this evening one hundred and seventeen Yankee officers, and arrangements will have to be made for them to share your quarters," was Captain Sennes's announcement.

We made hasty preparations to receive the "fresh fish." They ranked from second lieutenant up to colonel. Such a motley and reckless lot I never met before. All had been captured inside the rebel forts when the mine was exploded at Petersburg. We were uncomfortably crowded for room with so many men, and Captain Sennes proposed to the old prisoners that we should sign a parole and return to our quarters on the first floor. We readily agreed to it. On our part, we were not to escape by tunnelling, or from the yard; on their part, our door was to be left open, with liberty to go into the yard when necessary, and also one hour in the morning and afternoon for recreation.

Williams and Porter had been released from irons. The six officers highest in rank among the new arrivals were assigned to the rooms which they had vacated, and granted the same privileges as we. On Main Street was the printing establishment of Ball & Keating. The building extended across the rear of our yard. We were greatly surprised to see a number of young ladies taking a good view of the prisoners from a second-story window. The rebs had gotten scared, and had moved the Bureau of Printing and Engraving from Richmond to Columbia. Ball & Keating's establishment was selected for the printing of the Confederate currency. The money was not worth stealing. An ordinary burglar could have taken away a cart-load of the notes. At night the money was left loose in the different rooms, the same as a lot of hand-bills in a common printing-office. The lady employés, as a means of recreation, would gaze at the Yankee hirelings in the prison-yard. A number of the privates had no coats or shirts, and were barefoot. The sight must have been very interesting.

When the officers were in the yard the privates had to remain in the barracks. That was the time that those young ladies from Virginia showed their good breeding. If one of us happened to get within spitting distance of a window, up would go their noses and down would come the saliva. At first we were inclined to be angry, but that was just what those females liked, so we changed our tactics, and threw kisses back when they spat. By that means the spitting was stopped. Every day we would hear exciting news from different sources.

What interested us most came direct from the Secretary of the Confederate navy. He authorized some gentlemen to make arrangements for a special exchange of prisoners. They called upon us and made the proposition that two naval officers should be paroled and sent to Washington to see if an exchange of naval prisoners, regardless of rank or numbers, could be effected. Lieutenant-Commanders Williams and Prendergast were given the mission. Both were given paroles for thirty days. If our Government consented to the proposition, they were to remain North; if not, they were to return to Richmond within a specified time. All the necessary documents were given to them, and they were started for Richmond the next day and taken to our lines on a flag-of-truce boat. Inside the thirty days we were notified that the exchange would be made. Great was the joy among our party at the prospect of soon returning home. It was soon known in Columbia that we were to be exchanged. Then I became mixed up in a mysterious affair which I have never been able to solve. Captain Sennes came to our room with a woman.

"Mr. Thompson, this lady has an order from the commandant to see you."

He then went out. The lady introduced herself as Mrs. Hall, of Washington, D. C. She had been South during the war; her husband was in Washington, and she had not been able to hear from him, and "would I be kind enough to deliver a letter to him?"

"Certainly." I was willing to help her in any way possible. We conversed a short time on ordinary topics.

"Do you know Colonel Dent?"

"No, I have never heard of such a person."

"Why, he is General Grant's brother-in-law, and is confined in this jail."

"Well, that is news to me. No one ever knew of his being here."

"It is a fact. He is confined on the top floor with the criminals, and I see him very often. He gave me a number of letters which he wishes taken to General Grant. Will you take them?"

"Yes, provided you answer a few questions. How did you know my name?"

"Through a lady who knew you while you were in the hospital."

"Why do you select me to carry letters for a man about whom I know nothing?"

"Because you were recommended to me."

"Very well, I will take them, provided I am allowed to know their contents. It seems strange to me that Colonel Dent should be confined in this jail as a criminal and not one of us Yankee prisoners know anything about it."

She assured me that he was Grant's brother-in-law, and had been arrested for some transaction about a plantation near New Orleans. There were several letters in the package, a petition to the Governor of Wisconsin, and a long letter written in short-hand. "He was a good Democrat, a loyal citizen.—See that my land in Wisconsin is not sold for non-payment of taxes," are some of the extracts. The others related to family affairs. The short-hand notes I could not read. What the petition was for I have forgotten. Mrs. Hall then presented me with a finely embroidered silk tobacco-pouch. Thanking me for my kindness, she bade me good-bye. When, afterward, I thought the affair over, I came to the conclusion that the letters were only a subterfuge to draw my suspicions from the short-hand notes. Not a word had been said in the letters about the cause of his arrest or about his being confined as a criminal. As I had promised to deliver the packet, I concluded to take the risk of getting myself in trouble with the Confederate authorities. They had a habit of searching the prisoners before crossing the line.[E]

[E] A number of years afterward, I was confined in the prison in Jefferson City, Mo. At that place guards were kept on the walls night and day. Convicts were selected as night watchmen for the different shops. It was my good fortune to be watchman in the saddle-tree shop. At that time Colonel John A. Joyce and General Williams—members of the Whisky Ring during Grant's administration—were serving a sentence of two years each. Joyce was cell-housekeeper in the negroes' building during the daytime, and Williams was storekeeper. Every evening they would come to my shop, and a pot of good coffee would be cooked on the stove. A couple of hours would be pleasantly passed in talking over past events. Generals Grant and Babcock were frequently mentioned in connection with the Whisky Ring. I told them all about Colonel Dent's being confined in the Columbia jail, and asked if they knew anything about the circumstances. Both of them commenced laughing; then the subject was dropped.

CHAPTER XXV
LIBBY PRISON

SQUADS of naval prisoners frequently passed through Columbia on their way to Richmond. At last orders were given for us to be ready at four o'clock the next morning. There was no sleeping that night in our room. Four of the guards were detailed to escort us to Libby Prison. As we left the jail, the army officers came to the windows and gave us three cheers and a "tiger." They little imagined then how soon they would have their own freedom. It was not long afterward until Sherman's "bummers" captured the city. The prisoners escaped from the jail before the rebs could remove them. As our troops entered the city the ex-prisoners found plenty of willing hands to help them set fire to the jail, city hall, and treasury buildings.

The first part of our journey was made in passenger coaches. In North Carolina we were changed to box-cars. When we got to Virginia travelling became worse; the train had to move very slowly. The Yankee cavalry had destroyed all the roads as much as possible. At one place, for a distance of thirty miles, not a house or a fence-rail could be seen. Twisted railroad iron was quite abundant. The only wood visible was the stumps of telegraph-poles in the ground. We were eight days in getting to Richmond, and well tired out with the trip. We were taken to the provost-marshal's office and thence to Libby Prison. Our squad was the last to arrive. About seventy-five officers and five hundred sailors and marines comprised all the Yankee naval prisoners. The sailors were confined at the extreme end of the building, a brick wall separating us. We had plenty of room for exercise in that big warehouse. The army officers had not taken all their companions with them when they went to Charleston, as we soon found out to our dismay. Every crack in the floor of that prison was filled with vermin, and the largest and finest specimens of the pest that could be found in the whole United States. In Columbia we had not been troubled with vermin, but in Libby it was impossible to get rid of them. The most of our spare time was devoted to hunting for game in our clothing, and no one ever complained about having bad luck. We were expecting almost hourly to be put on a flag-of-truce boat. Day after day passed, with no signs of our leaving. An old negro who brought in our rations of corn-bread informed us that the exchange might not take place, as Ben Butler was doing all he could to prevent it. General Ben Butler, or "Beast Butler," as he was called by the rebs, had command of the troops at City Point. Through neglect on his part to carry out the plan of the campaign he got "bottled up" by the rebels and probably prolonged the war. We had positive information that the naval rebel prisoners were on the boat at City Point, but why Butler should interfere was an enigma to us. It was a peculiarity of his to be always on the wrong side of the fence.

Master's Mate William Kitching, being desirous of having conversation with one of the boat's crew, had removed a couple of bricks from the partitions which separated the officers from the sailors. He told some of the men to pass the word for all of his men to come to the aperture. Much to his surprise he was informed that all the men belonging to his boat had died at Andersonville. Not one of the thirteen sailors were living. The other officers went to the hole and called for their men also. Only a very few answered to their names. Out of the sixteen sailors captured with me only three answered. About seventy-five per cent of the sailors had died in the different prisons. What puzzled us all was the fact of there being so many prisoners that none of us could identify. The men must have had consultation among themselves, as during the afternoon the situation of affairs was fully explained to us. Information had been received at the different prisons that the sailors were to be exchanged. They originated a plan to help all the soldiers possible. Sailors gave their most intimate friends the names of their deceased shipmates, the names of the ships, where and when captured, the names of the officers, and, in fact, all information that would be useful. The scheme had been successful, so far. They were told to continue the deception, and the officers would assist them in doing so. We had been in Libby three weeks and nothing definite was known, and we might go back South for all we knew.

About nine in the evening the stairs leading to the second floor were lowered.[F] One officer was called by name and taken into the office, and when he returned another was called, and so on, until all of us had been interviewed by the notorious Major Turner. The name of our ship, where and when captured, how many men we had, and a lot of other questions were asked. That racket continued until about three o'clock in the morning. Each of us had asked him about our prospects of being exchanged. "That is an affair about which I know nothing," was his answer. Of course, none of us thought about sleeping that night. Walking the floor and discussing the situation suited us better under the circumstances. About four o'clock there was more excitement. A day's ration of food was issued to each one. It consisted of two small pieces of corn-bread, and of mighty poor quality. At five o'clock that evening, Major Turner, and his equally notorious clerk, Ross, came to the head of the stairs. Our names were called, and each one sent down to the hall. An engineer's name was called, but that gentleman was ordered to stand by the door. When the list was exhausted the door was locked and the engineer left in the room. It was afterward learned that he stated to Turner that he belonged to an army transport. We were formed in line, in squads of four, facing the door. At six o'clock in the evening the doors were opened, and the order, "Forward, march," given.

[F] The stairs were hung on heavy hinges, and every night they would be hoisted up by a pulley, similar to a trap-door.

Outside was a strong escort of rebels. Our hearts were fairly in our mouths for a short time. If we turned for the left it would be for the flag-of-truce boat; if to the right, it meant an indefinite stay in prison. It was the "left," and all doubts were removed—we were going home! The sailors were brought out and followed in our rear. It was an interesting trip down the James River. We had a fine view of the rebel batteries. Three iron-clads were passed, and several pontoon bridges across the river had to be opened on our approach. The most interesting thing was the sunken obstructions, with the secret channels. Considerable skill was required to get the boat through them. The guns from Grant's and Lee's batteries could be plainly heard. Next in view were the rebel shells exploding high in air over Dutch Gap, Ben Butler's celebrated canal. Finally we espied some Yankee pickets, then came Aiken's Landing. The boat was fastened to the dock, and all went on shore and waited for the Commissioners of Exchanges to receive us. In a short time Major Mumford arrived. He was on horseback, and a flag of truce was stuck in his boot-leg. His salutation was:

"Boys, the ambulance will be here in a few minutes with the Confederates. You can either ride or walk, but get over to our boat as soon as you can, as the exchange may yet fall through."

As soon as the rebel prisoners came in sight we started off. Walking was good enough for us. What a contrast between the two parties! The rebel officers were all dressed in new Confederate uniforms—probably furnished by rebel sympathizers in the North—and the sailors all had good clothing, and were healthy in appearance. They also seemed happy about going home, even if they were bidding good-bye to coffee and tea. The least said about our party the better. We were only sorry that we had not time to catch a few pecks of vermin for the others to take back to the Confederate States of America.

On the rebel boat there was a brass band, and, as a parting compliment, they regaled us with the old familiar tune, "Then you'll remember me." There was a large bend in the river below Aiken's Landing, and our boat was quite a distance around the bend. We walked about a mile and a half across the strip of land, many of the disabled sailors following us in ambulances. On the dock were a large number of trunks, with a sentry guarding them. We were told that it was the baggage belonging to the rebel officers. Quite a number of our party made a rush for the trunks, with the intention of dumping them into the river. The guard said, "Go ahead, boys, I won't stop you," but Major Mumford advised them not to do it, as it might cause serious trouble. Then all went on board our boat, the Martha Washington. Several barrels of steaming hot coffee were ready.

"Boys, help yourselves. Crackers and cheese in the boxes!"

In a short time the Sanitary Commission boat came alongside. Clothing was furnished to all, and anything that could be done for the men was done cheerfully. Nothing was too good for the ex-prisoners. Surgeons were busy attending to the sick.

Scurvy and bowel complaints were the most common trouble. The officers were assigned to the after cabin, and the men were all given comfortable beds. From Libby to the Martha Washington made a wonderful change in our spirits. No one, to see us then, would recognise us as the miserable set of beings of a few hours past. In the cabin we had a fine dinner set before us, and bottles of whisky galore.

"Gentlemen, drink plenty of whisky while eating," were the orders from the surgeon.

The captain apologized for the lack of some extras that had been intended for us. The rebels had been on the boat for nearly three weeks, luxuriating on our provisions while we were enjoying ourselves in Libby. Secretary of War Stanton and "Beast Butler" brought about the event, they being opposed to the exchange. In the afternoon we steamed down the river. I had an interview with Major Mumford, and told him briefly about Colonel Dent.

"Yes, the colonel is a prisoner in the South. He is also Grant's brother-in-law."

"Well, I have a packet of letters from him to General Grant. How can I deliver them to him?"

"Give them to me. Grant is now at City Point. The boat will stop there, and I will see that he gets them," he replied.

I then handed him the package. He never asked me a single question in regard to Colonel Dent, and he did not give me a chance to ask him any questions. That ended the affair as far as I was concerned.

We stopped at City Point for half an hour on our way to Fortress Monroe. During the trip I had conversations with many of the sailors. They had suffered terribly during their imprisonment. Insufficient food and exposure had caused much sickness. Some of them had slept on the bare ground for months without any shelter. Nearly all had the scurvy. That any of them had lives to be exchanged was a miracle. The soldiers were very exultant at the success of their ruse in getting through the lines, and well they might be, for to-day there are seventeen thousand graves of their fellow-prisoners at Andersonville. Quite a number of sick men were also on the boat, having been sent from different hospitals in the South. The rebs thought that was the easiest way to get rid of them. We stopped at Fortress Monroe for a short time, and then proceeded to Annapolis, Md., and early next morning we were landed at the Naval Academy wharf. Sixteen men had died on that short trip from Aiken's Landing.

The sailors were cared for by the proper officials, and the officers were given transportation to Washington. Then I was a free man, after having been a prisoner of war for three hundred and eleven days.

CHAPTER XXVI
A FREE MAN AGAIN

I TOOK the first train for Washington, arriving there late at night. Going to the Metropolitan Hotel, I registered myself as from Columbia, S. C. The clerk looked at me for a moment, and asked if I had any baggage.

"Neither baggage nor money," I replied.

He commenced laughing, and told a bellboy to show me up to a room. I remained in Washington two days. My written report was made out; then I reported in person to Gideon Welles, the Secretary of the Navy. He was a fine old gentleman, and expressed his joy at the exchange being made. I have already narrated the particulars regarding Captain Gregory and his reports. I was instructed to go home, report my arrival, give my address, and await orders. My next visit was to the Fourth Auditor, for some of the back pay due me. In a short time I had some much-needed respectable clothing. As yet I had not fully recovered from the typhoid fever. My hair was dead, and rapidly falling out. A barber was consulted, and he discovered that a new crop had commenced to grow. So the old hair was cut off even with the new. Mrs. Hall's husband was then next in order. Upon inquiry, I found that he was a cheap gambler, and not in town just then, so I left his letter with some of his friends.

I arrived in New York on Sunday morning, and went to my wife's last address. She had changed quarters to another locality. On going there, I was informed that she was in a certain boarding-house in Brooklyn. At that place I was directed to another boarding-house. Finally I found the young lady. Our child had died three months previously. During our conversation I said:

"Why, Annie, I only received two of your letters while I was in prison."

"That is all I wrote to you," she very innocently replied.

Before leaving Boston on the brig Perry, I had made an allotment of fifty dollars per month to her, which she received from a naval agent on the first of each month. Well, that frugal little wife, to use a slang expression, was "dead broke," and in arrears for her board bill. I was happy to be back with her, so I had no fault to find. Theatres and pleasure trips were in order and my past miseries forgotten. In due time I received all my back pay. My clothing had been sent home from the Perry, and a sword and a few other articles were all I had to purchase for my new outfit.

Orders were received for me to report to Commander John C. Hall, for duty on board the United States steamer Nereus, at the Brooklyn Navy Yard. The Nereus was a large screw steamer, with splendid accommodations for sailors and officers. The captain and executive were regulars, the other officers were volunteers. The acting master was a navigating officer. Four ensigns were watch officers. Our quarters consisted of a large ward-room, with state-rooms on each side. The latter were furnished with single berths, and sets of drawers underneath, a combination dressing-case and desk, and a stationary wash-stand. Coloured ordinary seamen were detailed as ward-room boys, one for each officer. Their duties were to take care of the state-rooms and wait on the table, for which service they received nine dollars per month extra, paid by the officers. The steward and cook were paid as petty officers by the Government. One hundred dollars were paid by each of the officers as initiation fee and mess fund on joining the vessel, and afterward a *pro rata* of the expense was charged to each. There was quite a contrast between the Nereus and the Perry. The ward-room officers consisted of one lieutenant, one master, four ensigns, paymaster, surgeon, and chief engineer. The master's mate and second and third engineers each had separate mess-rooms in the steerage.

Seven of the officers were ex-prisoners of war. A few months afterward Captain Howell stated that we were the wildest lot he ever commanded; it only took a short time for him to form his opinion, however. The vessel was ordered to the squadron at Cape Haitien, Hayti, West Indies. The Panama steamers had to be convoyed through the Mariguana Passage, thence between Cape Maisi, Cuba, and San Nicolas la Mole, Hayti, to Navassa Island. The rebel steamer Alabama had captured one of the Panama boats, securing eight hundred thousand dollars in gold bullion, and had bonded the steamer for the same amount, to be paid when the Confederacy gained its independence. Fort Fisher was to be attacked, and Captain Howell got permission to join the expedition with his vessel. All of us were pleased with the chance to pay up old scores with the rebels. The corn-meal was still rankling in our systems. Steam was gotten up, and, under charge of a pilot, we started for Sandy Hook. Before we got a hundred yards from the dock the trip very abruptly ended. The pilot ran too close to a large floating buoy, and the result was that one of the propeller blades caught the heavy chain by which the buoy was anchored. The engines were slowly reversed. It was of no use. That chain was there to stay, and we were securely fastened by the stern. I shall never forget that December night. It was my watch on deck from twelve to four in the morning. The thermometer was twenty-one degrees below zero, and I thought I would freeze to death. The men on deck I sent below out of the cold wind, but I had no place for shelter, as the deck was clear fore and aft.

The next day a submarine diver examined the propeller blade. The chain was jammed in between the stern-post and the centre of the screw. A floating derrick was fastened to our stern, the buoy and anchor were hoisted on it, and our vessel was thus taken into the dry dock. It was quite a job to free the chain. That little mishap detained us one week. We made another start and got to Fortress Monroe. Taking a monitor in tow, we went to Fort Fisher. Nearly all the expedition had arrived, and the bombardment was begun. That expedition was probably the worst "fizzle" of the whole war. There were over sixty ships in the fleet, each carrying from four to forty-four guns, besides several monitors carrying fifteen-inch guns. The total number of guns was about six hundred. The rebels considered Fort Fisher as being impregnable, and it was, beyond all doubt, a strong fort. It was built on a narrow strip of land between Cape Fear River and the ocean. There was an embankment over a mile in length, twenty-five feet thick and twenty feet high. About two thirds of it faced the sea; the other third ran across the strip of land as protection from land attack. Still stronger than these were the traverses, which prevented an enfilading fire. These were hills about forty feet in height, and broad and long in proportion, about twenty of them along the sea face of the fort. Inside of them were the bomb-proofs, large enough to shelter the whole garrison. In front of the works was a strong palisade. Between each of the traverses was mounted one or two large guns, none less than one-hundred-and-fifty pounders, all of the guns of English manufacture. One, in particular, was an enormous Armstrong gun, mounted on a rosewood carriage—a present from Sir William Armstrong, of England. Fort Castle and Fort Anderson also protected the Cape Fear River. The channel was filled with sunken torpedoes. Torpedoes were also buried in the sand in front of Fort Fisher. An immense mound, one hundred feet in height, was erected on the beach and a large gun mounted on the summit.

Now for a description of the whole affair in a plain and truthful manner. I have read many descriptions of the capture of Fort Fisher, and have seen pictures portraying it, but all were exaggerations. An old steamer, the Louisiana, was fitted up in imitation of a blockade-runner, and two hundred and fifteen tons of gunpowder were loaded in the hold. Fuses were connected with an exploding clockwork and the powder. It was supposed that such a quantity of powder exploding so near the fort would do great damage, besides killing all of the garrison. The idea was suggested by Ben Butler. General Grant had given Butler orders to send General Weitzel with five thousand troops for the capture of the fort, and afterward to capture Wilmington, so that Sherman could receive supplies for his army. Butler ignored the orders, and took personal command of the troops, leaving Weitzel at City Point. The squadron was at Fort Fisher on time. Butler with his troops had not arrived. Then began the trouble. Admiral Porter gave orders to explode the powder-boat, and all arrangements were quickly made. The squadron was to steam ten miles out at sea. All safety valves were to be opened, lest the concussion might cause the boilers to explode. Under cover of darkness the powder-boat was towed by the steamer Wilderness close to the fort. The clockwork was set, also a fire was laid in case the clockwork failed. The crew were taken off by the Wilderness. The clock arrangement proved a failure, but the fire, in time, caused an explosion. Not a particle of damage was done to the fort. We afterward learned that most of the Confederates were asleep, and some of them never heard the explosion. The next day Butler arrived with his transports. He was terribly angry about the powder-boat affair. In the meantime the fleet, by divisions, had formed a line of battle. The ironclads were close to the shore. Their fire was to be direct. The other ships were to fire at angles with the fort so as to make an enfilading fire as much as possible. The bombardment from so many guns was terrific. The Confederates were soon driven into the bomb-proofs. During the day nearly all their guns were dismounted. The next day was Christmas, 1864. Early in the morning the landing of the troops began. Every boat in the fleet was brought into requisition. A clear strip of land extended from the fort to the woods, about a mile in length. A spot near the centre of the clear space was selected as the best place for the troops to land. A heavy surf was running on the beach. Every time a boat-load was landed it was necessary for the crew to wade out into the surf with the boat, and, at the proper time, jump in and pull through the first breaker. If not quick enough, the boat would be keeled over and over, high up on the beach. Everything was progressing finely; no one doubted but that the fort would be captured before night. All the white troops were on shore. We were busily engaged in landing Butler's pet coloured troops. What was our astonishment on receiving orders to re-embark the troops and bring off the negroes first, and then Ben Butler's transports started immediately for Washington, with that gallant hero on board! A heavy gale of wind set in from the northeast and continued to increase in fury as the night approached; consequently the surf was getting worse and it was very difficult for the boats to get clear of the beach. Those "niggers" would rush for every boat and overload it, with the result that it would be swamped. If ever "niggers" got a cursing, they certainly got it that night. About midnight my boat was swamped three times in succession. I was thoroughly disgusted. The crew and I were well tired out. We had had nothing to eat since morning, our clothing was soaking wet from constantly being in the surf, and the cold wind was chilling our bodies. The boat was lifted up sideways and the water dumped out. Everything was made ready for a new start, but this time I held my revolver in hand:

"Now, the first nigger who attempts to get in my boat will be shot!" and I meant what I said. It was hard work for us to get through the surf, and I felt certain that no more troops could be taken off that night. It was very dark and cloudy. I steered for the lights which were on the Nereus. We had gone about half the distance when the boat suddenly capsized and dumped all hands into the water. What caused that mishap I could never find out; it has always been a puzzle to me. It was lucky that none of us was hurt. Our clothing was very heavy, and made it difficult for us to keep from sinking, especially in such a rough sea. My sword and revolver made additional weight for me. We managed to hold on to the boat occasionally. In a few minutes we heard the splashing of oars in the water, and, by yelling, we attracted the attention of the boat's crew. They carefully approached and pulled us out of the sea. The boat was one of the launches belonging to the frigate Wabash. They took our boat in tow and rowed us to the Nereus. I was the only officer on our vessel who got back with his boat not damaged. The others were all badly disabled, and were left on the beach. About seven hundred of the soldiers were left on shore, and there they had to remain for three days. All night long the division to which the Nereus belonged fired shells into the woods to prevent Confederate troops from Wilmington making any attempt to capture our men. When the gale abated they were embarked. The first attack on Fort Fisher had ended in a grand fizzle, simply because Butler and Porter were at loggerheads. The army transports went back to City Point. The men-of-war weighed anchor and started for Beaufort, S. C. The few guns that still remained mounted at Fort Fisher fired a parting salute, in derision at our departure.

CHAPTER XXVII
FORT FISHER

ON our arrival at Beaufort all was bustle and activity. Ammunition and coal were taken on board, the small boats repaired, and everything was made ready for another expedition. Porter was continually sending despatches to Washington. Butler was there in person. Between them there was a lively war of words. The new expedition sailed for Fort Fisher. During our absence the enemy had repaired the fort, and the garrison had been increased from six hundred to a thousand men. General Terry arrived with his transports, having on board five thousand white troops. The fort was bombarded, and the garrison driven into the bomb-proofs. Several of our hundred-pounder rifled guns exploded, doing considerable damage, and that class of guns was not used any more during the action. On the 14th of January the troops were all landed. On the 15th two thousand sailors and marines were also landed, each vessel sending a detachment. The quota from the Nereus was fifty men, Ensign Dayton and myself being in command. We received printed orders from Admiral Porter:

"When you get in the fort, if the rebels refuse to surrender, four seamen must take each rebel and throw him over the ramparts."

That is one extract. There was more in the same strain. The men had been notified in advance as to who had been detailed for the assaulting party, but not so the officers. When the men were ready to get into the boats, Dayton and I were called from our gun divisions and received orders to take charge of them.

Our preparations were hastily made; each of us took a ship's cutlass, revolver, and breech-loading carbine, and then filled our pockets with ammunition. The surgeon was on hand with a supply of tourniquets and bandages, which he jammed into our pockets while giving us brief lectures on the compression of arteries. In a short time the sailors were landed; the marines were detailed as sharp-shooters, each one having his knapsack as a portable breastwork. About one o'clock the army was ready for the assault in the rear end of the fort. The marines deployed to their position; the sailors moved up the beach in double column, the ships firing over us.

Some of the enemy came out of their bomb-proofs and kept continually firing into our columns. The beach was perfectly level, with no friendly trees or rocks to afford us any protection. Our destination was the sea face of the fort. To get there it was necessary to march two thirds of a mile parallel with the fort, and within easy range—a few hundred yards. We would willingly have gone a little more to the left if the Atlantic Ocean had permitted. Before getting to our proper position, a signal from the flagship ordered us to lie down on the beach. The shot and shell were whistling over our heads at a terrible rate, and sometimes an over-zealous gunner would make a slight error and drop them among our men instead of into the fort. Some of the enemy also made it interesting from their side of the fence. Quite a number was killed or wounded among our party. The water was splashed up in a lively way by the bullets. Strangely enough, every wounded sailor, if able, would crawl to the water and lie down, so that the surf, as it rolled up the beach, kept his body wet. It was low tide at the time, and, as we lay down on the wet sand, we soon became chilled through. Nearly two hours we remained in that position. A large gun just opposite me, inside the fort, still remained mounted. I noticed that the muzzle was elevated to aim at the fleet, but was gradually being depressed, so that it was in range with our men. The gunners could be seen putting in the powder and two stands of grape-shot. It was left in that position, and the gunners disappeared. One of our iron-clads was close inshore, just opposite the loaded gun. About every ten minutes they would fire a fifteen-inch, with a reduced charge of powder, consequently we could see every shell as it passed over us. They all went about five feet above the gun and exploded in the rear. Why they did not attempt to dismount it I cannot imagine. They certainly must have seen the enemy loading it.

A projectile from a rifled gun in the fleet got to tumbling "end over end" in the air. It landed within six feet of me. The sand flew in every direction, nearly blinding some of the men. For a few seconds we all felt nervous. If it was a percussion fuse shell the danger was past; if a time fuse, it would explode, and the only means of safety was to lie flat on the ground. To attempt to run away would be very dangerous. For a few seconds we all remained quiet. No hissing sound could be heard, and then the missile was examined, and proved to be a solid shot; but we were, for awhile, badly scared.

The soldiers could be seen beginning the attack at the rear of the fort. Then came Admiral Porter's terrible blunder. The signal was given for the fleet to "cease firing," then for the sailors to advance. We had quite a distance to go up the beach before making a "right face" and rushing into the fort. The Confederates had anticipated that very movement on our part, and were prepared for it. They rushed out of the bomb-proofs, and gave our troops a murderous fire of musketry without our being able to return the fire. Then the big gun was discharged, and it made a terrible gap in our column. The detachment just ahead of ours was almost annihilated as they received the full charge of grape-shot. Some of the men were thrown several feet into the air. Each of the grape-shot weighed three pounds. There must have been nearly a hundred in the charge, as it was a double load from a hundred-and-fifty pounder. About two hundred men near the head of the column had reached some low sand-dunes which protected them, but the men following them became panic-stricken, and fell back upon those in their rear. The whole column was thrown into disorder, and compelled to retreat, the enemy keeping up a heavy fire as we passed down the beach. As badly whipped as the sailors were, they deserved great credit for one thing: not a wounded shipmate was deserted; all were carried off. The dead were all dragged up above high-water mark, so that the tide would not carry their bodies out to sea. Had we marched up to our proper position, under cover of fire from the fleet, and the attack then been made, results would have been different, but being killed outright, through lack of good judgment, would discourage almost anybody! The plan of the attack was good. With the sailors assaulting the front and the soldiers the rear, the enemy would have been between two fires. Colonel Pennypacker, with his regiment, was inside the fort, the other regiments on the outside of the traverses; they were gradually driving the enemy back. Signals were made to the fleet where to throw their shells so as to avoid hitting our own troops. The sailors were reorganized, and manned the trenches across the open ground, to prevent re-enforcements to the Confederates coming from Wilmington. By that arrangement, a regiment armed with seven-shot repeating rifles was relieved and added to the assaulting party at the fort.

Night came on and the fight still continued. Signals by light were made to the fleet how to direct their fire. At one o'clock in the morning the battle was ended by the enemy surrendering. The last prop was knocked from under the Confederacy; their great source of supplies was cut off. Blockade-running was ended. General Sherman would have a new base of supplies. Richmond would soon have to be evacuated. The day the fort was captured, Ben Butler was in Washington, demonstrating to the authorities, theoretically, why Fort Fisher was impregnable. Captain Breeze and Lieutenants Cushing, Preston, and Porter, from the flagship Malvern, had command of the sailors. Preston and Porter were fellow-prisoners of mine at Columbia. Both were killed early in the attack, Preston by a shell from the fleet, and Porter by a bullet. Cushing, with all his bravery, was not the last officer of the retreat down the beach—not by long odds. It is now a matter of history that Captain Breese with two hundred sailors actually got inside the fort and remained there until nightfall. That is all bosh. The fact is, they were behind the sand-dunes when the panic occurred—it being much safer to remain there than to be running the gauntlet down to the sea. After dark they retreated in good order. If they had really got into the fort, I will guarantee that they would not have remained there very long. The sailor who got closest to the traverses was an ensign from the gunboat Sassacus, and he was killed. Ensign Dayton, my fellow-officer, had not been seen by me since we landed. When I next saw him it was on board the Nereus. He said he had been with Captain Breese. He received some very plain talk from me for not helping to look after our own men. There was enough to be attended to—the wounded to be sent to the vessel, the dead to be identified and buried, and, the most difficult job, to corral the live ones and get them off to the Nereus. They were scattered all over our newly acquired territory. It was not every day they could get ashore, and they were certainly making good use of their opportunities.

Early in the morning the dead sailors were laid side by side, forming a long row. Their caps, having the ship's name on in gilt letters, were placed on their breasts, and a slip of paper, giving his full name, was fastened to each man's shirt. It was a weird sight. All of them were fine-looking young men. I had placed the names on the men belonging to the Nereus, and went towards the fort, and as I got near the traverses I was nearly thrown off my feet by a sudden shaking of the ground; then I saw an immense conical-shaped mass of earth and timbers thrown high into the air; then a large circle of dust descended and covered everything in our vicinity. We all looked as if we had been pulled through a chimney. One of the magazines in the fort had blown up. The remnant of a Wisconsin regiment was stationed in the fort after its surrender, and the explosion killed nearly all.

Quite a number of us assisted in getting the dead and wounded from the ruins. At first it was supposed that a torpedo connected by wires with Fort Anderson had caused the disaster, but it was afterward decided that it had been an accident. The Confederate prisoners were then furnished with shovels, and forced to dig up a number of torpedoes that had been buried on the outside of the fortification.

No wonder our troops had hard work to capture that place, for, by the peculiar construction of the interior defences, it was easy to repel the attacking forces. Towards evening I succeeded in getting the survivors of our detachment on board the Nereus, and was very particular about having our quota of small-arms sent with them—carbines, revolvers, and cutlasses, fifty-two of each. No questions were asked about their being the same ones we took ashore with us. The gunner's report was "All arms returned," and nothing more was necessary. The fact that Dayton brought his extra equipments unknown to me was not commented on.

My report, accounting for all the men, was given to the executive officer, and then I had something to eat. I went to bed, having had no sleep for thirty-six hours, but I had enough glory to last me for a long time. The next night the rebels blew up Forts Caswell and Anderson, and beat a hasty retreat for Wilmington. General Terry soon after captured the latter place. The hospital transport came alongside the Nereus and took off our wounded men, and I have never seen or heard of one of them since. Our anchor was weighed and we returned to Beaufort for a supply of ammunition and coal, and as soon as possible started for the West Indies to join our squadron.

About eight days after our departure from Beaufort we sighted Turks Island, and, going through the Mariguana Passage, we soon had a view of the high mountains of the Island of Haiti. The weather was fine and quite a contrast to that of New York. The awnings were spread to protect us from the hot sun, and heavy clothing was discarded.

CHAPTER XXVIII
THE ISLAND OF HAITI

CAPE HAITIEN is a queer little town built on the shore of a bay at the foot of a very high mountain. When the French possessed the place it was called "La petite Paris," but an earthquake tumbled all the buildings, and generally wrecked the whole place. A great many of the ruins still remain. Some of the stone was utilized for new habitations, but most of it was left where it had fallen.

The negroes had no ambition to restore the place to its former grandeur, and only a few white men were to be found among its inhabitants. Mahogany, logwood, and coffee were the only exports, and those only in small quantities. We had arrived on a Sunday afternoon, and several of us went on shore to visit the American consul, as an act of courtesy, and then strolled through the town. Whisky was not allowed on board a man-of-war, and it was quite natural for us to want a drink on our arrival in a foreign country. Stopping at the only hotel, we ordered a "brandy smash," and it nearly paralyzed the whole crowd. The atmosphere was quite warm, and so was the brandy and water. There was no ice in the whole town, and of all the mixed drinks I ever had that was the worst. We had received some gold money from the paymaster, and a five-dollar piece was given in payment for the aforesaid drinks. Well, the change that was returned almost finished what the "smash" had not quite done, for about sixty-four one-dollar bills were counted out, each printed on bright yellow paper, about five by seven inches in size. "Une Gourde"—meaning "one dollar"—was printed in large and small letters all over the face of the note, and then, in French, something about its redemption at a certain period.

The landlord was a Frenchman and had learned to speak English while on board an American whaling vessel. He gave us considerable information about the town, and also advised us to have our gold exchanged for his Haitien currency, so we each got five dollars' worth from him. The "gourdes" were at a discount of ninety-three per cent, making each one worth seven cents in gold. Such a roll of bills as we received! The bundles had to be put in our coat-tail pockets, no other place being large enough to hold them. The only amusement in town that would take place that night was a masquerade ball. Each of our drinks came to one "gourde," rather cheap for brandy. We bade our host adieu until evening and returned to the Nereus. Lieutenant Mullen, the surgeon, paymaster, three ensigns, and three engineers made up a party to "take in" the masquerade.

Special permit was required to be absent after sundown, as we were under war regulations. No time was lost in getting to the hotel. The landlord piloted us to the ballroom. Two "gourdes" were charged each for admission. A large store with a brick floor was the extemporized ballroom. In one corner, on a platform, was the orchestra, and four "niggers" with clarionets composed it. In another end of the room was the office, with a window opening into the store-room, that place being transformed into a temporary barroom, the window-sill being the bar over which the drinks were served. Lieutenant Mullen belonged in Baltimore, Md., and he had no use for "niggers" under any circumstances, but he did like liquor, and it seemed to have very little effect on him. When the music struck up we all chose partners, with the exception of Mullen, that gentleman selecting one side of the window-sill and keeping it all night. My partner was neatly dressed and genteel in appearance, and, as she was closely masked, I could not tell whether she was pretty or not. She wore white kid gloves, and, as part of her wrists was exposed, I could see by the smooth skin that she was young, and probably a quadroon. That girl had the advantage of me, as I had no mask, and she knew with whom she was dancing while I did not. However, both of us seemed satisfied, for we were partners in every waltz.

About two in the morning we had to leave our coloured partners, for the boat was to be at the landing for us at that hour. In the streets there were no lamps. A light, drizzling rain made the darkness more intense. Our most direct route was by a street facing the beach. A number of warehouses had large quantities of logwood piled in front, and the pieces were very crooked and lying in all positions. The doctor and I were walking together. His vision was concentrated on the logwood, and finally he expressed himself:

"Say, Thompson, did you ever see so many anchors piled up in a street before?"

Of course Cape Haitien had a military dock for the men-of-war boats to land at. On the shore end was a small guard-house, and as we passed it I noticed a light through the open doorway. Looking inside, I saw several Haitien soldiers sleeping soundly. In one corner of the shanty was a most primitive lamp—a glass tumbler partly filled with water, and a small quantity of oil on the top of it with a lighted wax taper floating in it. Here was an opportunity to make myself a benefactor to my fellow-officers. Without any hesitation I stole the lamp.

"Hello, gentlemen, allow me to carry a light down the wharf for you!"

Just then an engineer named Patterson gave my hand a knock, and away went the whole illuminating apparatus. My eyes were blinded by the sudden change from light to darkness. I walked about three steps, and off the dock I went head first into the water. The unexpected immersion improved my eyesight wonderfully, and when I got back on the dock I could walk without a light. Patterson thought the whole affair a huge joke. When we reached the Nereus it came my turn to laugh. Naval etiquette requires officers to go up the companion-ladder according to rank—the seniors first. Mr. Patterson, being lowest in grade, was to go up last, and by some means he lost balance and fell out of the boat; when he came to the surface of the water, some of the sailors pulled him into the boat. He was not at all funny when he reached the deck.

Grasping his hand, I said, "Shipmate, I feel sorry for you."

That was our only night on shore. Captain Howell was of the opinion that we could have pleasure enough during the daylight in the future. Hardly a day passed that some of us was not raising "Old Ned." After supper we would sit in the ward-room and relate our adventures, and some of them were comical. By no means could we get into high society in that town. We were politely referred to as persons of unfortunate colour. That was the only country I ever visited where a white man, if he behaved himself, was not as good as a "nigger." The east half of the island is the Republic of Haiti, formerly belonging to France, and the language spoken is French.

The western part is the Republic of San Domingo, formerly belonging to Spain, and the language spoken is Spanish. The whole island had, at one time, been very prosperous, but the slaves had formed a conspiracy, and in one night had massacred all the whites and gained their independence, France and Spain never being able to reconquer them. The negroes became quite indolent. Very little clothing is needed in that warm climate, and fruit, growing with little cultivation, provides them with food. Revolutions are of frequent occurrence. On the 1st, 11th, and 21st of each month two of our ships would sail from Cape Haitien to meet the California mail steamers, one going north to Turks Island, the other south to Navassa Island. Our first trip was to the latter place. The island was about three miles in circumference and almost inaccessible. It was the breeding-place of sea-birds. A company belonging to Baltimore, Md., had possession, and were shipping the guano to different parts of Europe. We arrived some hours before the mail steamer was due.

A kedge anchor was fastened to a heavy rope and dropped overboard, fish-lines were brought into service, and the sport began. The only question with us was, What kind of fish will the next be? Such a variety I never saw in my life in any part of the world—all different sorts, sizes, and shapes were landed on deck. The steamer came in sight and our anchor was pulled up. When the steamer came close by, a boat was sent to her with mail from our fleet, two cakes of ice were presented to us, and the vessel started for the passage. Before the mail steamer, being much the faster boat, was out of sight, it being of no use to convoy a vessel we could not see, we did the next best thing—returned to Cape Haitien. The steamer at Turks Island adopted the same tactics, with the exception of receiving the mail instead of sending it.

The Neptune, Galatea, Proteus, and Nereus certainly had an easy time on convoy duty.

CHAPTER XXIX
I LEAVE THE SEA AND GO WEST

ABOUT the 1st of April I sent in my resignation. I had become tired of sailor life, the war was nearly ended, and the fact that I was married made me desirous to make a living on dry land. It was a foolish whim of mine to throw away such a good opportunity, especially after having advanced so far in my chosen profession. A fresh supply of naval stores was needed on the Nereus, and for that reason we were ordered to Key West, then to return to Cape Haitien. We went first to Navassa and met the mail steamer, and the letter containing my resignation went in that mail pouch. We then steered for Cape Mayzi, at the eastern end of Cuba, and, going around the cape, we sailed west along the coast. Morro Castle was sighted, and we entered the harbour of Havana. I was well acquainted with the city, but everything appeared different to me then. The United States naval uniform allowed me to visit places where formerly, in common seaman's garb, I should have been denied.

The lottery-ticket venders were as busy as of yore, but, somehow, I did not feel like patronizing them. I drew the shares of only one prize in my life, but plenty of blanks. A drawing took place while I was in the city, and a number of us went to see it. The drawing was in a building like a theatre. Prizes ranging from two hundred and fifty thousand dollars down to one hundred dollars were in the wheel. The numbers of the tickets were in another. A remarkable audience was in the seats; rich and poor, black and white, and of all nationalities. Great excitement prevailed until the numbers of all the great prizes were called out. Then the crowd began to leave. Such low prizes as twenty thousand and ten thousand dollars interested no one.

We remained one week in Havana and then sailed for Key West, eighty miles distant; we were only a few hours at sea, and then our anchor was dropped in Key West harbour. That place had changed wonderfully since my last visit. From an indolent little fishing village and the home of the "wreckers" it had become a lively little town. The army and navy were well represented, and there was hustle and hurry everywhere. Wine and beer were the only liquors allowed on the island, and the beer cost fifty cents a bottle, so there must have been quite a profit for somebody. Our stores had been placed on board, then the coal was received, and when the bunkers were nearly filled it was discovered that some of the lower deck beams were getting out of place. An order was given to have the Nereus examined, and a report was given of her condition. The news of the surrender of Lee was received, and quite a celebration of the event took place. Next came the news of the assassination of President Lincoln.

The Nereus was condemned as "unfit for service," and orders were given for us to return to New York. About the 10th of May the Nereus arrived at the Brooklyn Navy Yard, and her career as a man-of-war was ended. The paymaster received notice from the Fourth Auditor at Washington that my resignation had been accepted on the 17th day of April, and he said that he would have my account made out at once. I informed the gentleman that he would do no such thing, and that when I should receive notice through Captain Howell that my resignation had been accepted I should be released from service, and not before then. Captain Howell decided that I was right. The acceptance had been sent to Cape Haitien, and I was in New York. The Nereus was put out of commission and the crew discharged. All the officers, except myself, were "detached" and granted two months' leave of absence. I was placed on waiting orders. The Neptune, Proteus, and Galatea had also arrived from Cape Haitien. My discharge should have been on one of those vessels, but no one knew anything about the missing document.

Our vessel had left Cape Haitien just in time to miss exciting scenes. A revolution had taken place, and it was the city against the whole republic. The English gunboat got mixed up in the mêlée and bombarded the city. The women took refuge on the men-of-war during the bombardment. The man-of-war Bulldog ran on a reef in the harbour and became a wreck. The English Government dismissed the captain for acting without authority, and the sailing-master met the same fate for losing the vessel. After waiting a reasonable time, I wrote to the Secretary of the Navy as to how I was situated, but received no reply. Captain Howell was in Washington, so I sent him a letter about my circumstances. He attended to the case personally, and in a few days I received a copy of the acceptance of my resignation on April 17, 1865. The copy was dated June 14th, and I received my pay to that date. I then got a position as watchman in the Brooklyn Navy Yard at sixty dollars a month. Renting a suite of rooms, I furnished them nicely and settled down to life on shore with my wife. A child was soon born to comfort our household.

I was finally, at my own request, transferred to the harbour patrol boat. There were nine of us, divided into three crews, twelve hours on duty and twenty-four hours off. River pirates and deserters were our special game.

The war was ended, and that stopped desertion. The purchased gunboats were sold at auction, and then there was nothing left for the river pirates to plunder. Alas! our services were no longer needed, and we were all discharged. Next I got a situation in the navy yard machine-shops, for I was ambitious to become a first-class machinist. Busy times were over, and men returning from the war overstocked the labour market. A great reduction was ordered in all the navy yard machine-shops, and, of course I, being a late arrival, had to be discharged with the first lot. Gradually what money I had saved up was used for necessary living expenses. Rent and provisions were still at war prices, consequently I soon found myself dead broke, and with no prospects of obtaining employment.

I came to the conclusion that there was no hope of obtaining employment in New York. Selling part of my furniture, I raised a few dollars; then taking Horace Greeley's advice—"Go West, young man, go West!"—I left New York, and have been away just thirty-two years—1898.

The manuscript breaks off abruptly at the time when Thompson moved West. Almost from that change began his criminal career. It is known that he served two terms in the penitentiary at Joliet, Ill., the last one being for a period of twelve years. Both sentences were for burglary. In his manuscript he refers to an experience in the prison at Jefferson City, Mo., and it is also known that he died in prison in another State.

In the last writing of Thompson, he solemnly affirmed his belief in a "just and merciful God." To that divine justice and mercy let us, having learned our own lesson from his life, leave him, judging not, lest we be judged.

THE END